Brenda Courtie was born in Bootle. Growing up in bomb-scarred dockland, her idea of Heaven was a suburb called Hatton Hill, where there were houses with gardens, electric light and indoor toilets, and a church with stained-glass windows named St Paul's. Now she is married to the vicar of St Paul's, and in the intervals between being 'cook, cleaner and secretary' and the mother of two teenage boys, she writes for newspapers and magazines and broadcasts on Radio Merseyside in the character of the Scouse housewife Mrs Gladys Tidings — Glad Tidings to her friends! This is her first book.

Brenda Courtie

❋ NOT QUITE HEAVEN

TRIANGLE

First published 1984
Triangle
SPCK
Holy Trinity Church
Marylebone Road
London NW1 4DU

British Library Cataloguing in Publication Data

Courtie, Brenda
  Not quite heaven.
  1. Church of England—Great Britain—
Clergy   2. Clergymen's wives—Great Britain
—Religious life
  I. Title
  248.4'83043   BV4395

ISBN 0-281-04101-6

Typeset by Pioneer, East Sussex
Printed in Great Britain by
the Anchor Press, Tiptree

Contents

1 Heaven as Seen from Bootle 1

2 Growing up a Methodist 8

3 Jazz and Jesus 15

4 Toxteth to Oxfordshire 26

5 Darkness to Light 36

6 Coal-tips, Kids and a Calling 44

7 Singing Together in Durham 56

8 Living Together in Durham 69

9 Liverpool: Same City, New Life 80

10 A Living on a Hill 93

11 Hello, Glad Tidings! 104

12 Not Quite Heaven, But . . . 110

Chapter 1

❊ Heaven as Seen from Bootle

Funny things, my knees. Sort of fair weather friends. Most of the time they're on my side, supporting me when I stand or walk, or pumping like pistons to propel me on my bike, or getting me down to pray or scrub with never a hint of a twinge.

But comes the time when I get up in front of an audience and the knees go on strike. They quiver with fear and mutter, 'Oh no! Count us out. You're on your own for this one!'

Fortunately, it's only ever temporary. A quick psychological lecture on 'stiff upper lip' and 'backbone' and 'they don't throw Christians to the lions any more' and we're friends again.

This particular evening we'd been through the routine with a bit more hassle than usual. Finally I sat down and thought to myself: 'Well, it wasn't too bad, I suppose. The knees did stop knocking eventually.'

It was my first talk to our ladies' meeting and my first talk as a vicar's wife. One of a million hurdles I'd clambered over since my husband began his training for the Church of England priesthood. He was a schoolmaster then, and we'd been married nine years already and had two small sons.

My hand was still shaking, though, as I drank the cup of tea the secretary brought me. Was maturity so much of an advantage, I wondered? Would I have been more or less nervous ten years younger?

A motherly lady pulled her chair alongside mine. 'That was lovely!' she said with a smile.

'Well, you said "tell us something about yourself"', I answered, half apologetically.

'It took me right back, it did. In fact, I remember the day your father died. My mother met your Gran and came back to tell me the news.'

I know I smiled back at her, because I'll never forget the enormous effort it took, as the tea churned in my stomach. She remembered! There were people here who remembered more than I could. I was three years old when my father died and I have no specific recollection of the event.

'And fancy you coming back here after all these years,' she chattered on, shaking her head in gentle disbelief. 'Fancy! And married to our new vicar! Who'd have guessed!'

Who indeed?

So much water had rushed beneath so many bridges. At what point had the river of my life set its course for this particular scene? John's ordination? Our marriage? My conversion? Or was the course set even earlier? The Methodist youth club? Childhood picnics on this very spot? Yes, maybe that was when my life began its hike towards this point.

But it could have been even earlier.

My father was killed in the last year of the Second World War, in a truck-loading accident at his army camp just two miles from home. He'd never even been abroad to fight. My brother was born three weeks later and, after the street party on VE Day, we settled down to our new family life in what was a fairly common post-war situation — a young widowed mum with a couple of kids. It was a traumatic change for a little girl who weeks earlier had been the only child of two doting parents.

The Bootle street where we lived had changed a bit too. The blitz on the Liverpool North Docks had also flattened row upon row of the little terraced houses. Ours was typical of those that survived, a tiny, gas-lit, two-up-and-two-down, with many missing roof slates, crooked doors and windows, shattered quarry tile floors, and a matching draughty privy down the yard.

The bottom end of the street between us and the railway

had gone, bombed flat, and behind us the little streets between our house and the docks had also disappeared. From our back bedroom window I could look out across an acre of debris to the North Terminal of the overhead railway and the cranes and warehouses of the Gladstone Dock.

However, teetering on the very edge of dereliction and collapse it might be, but inside our little house was still home. The two downstairs rooms were dominated by their enormous black iron ranges, shining like jet. There was no wallpaper, just coloured distemper, and no electricity, just pendant gas lamps with their fragile mantles and hissing yellow light. The front living-room range had a tall brass-rimmed fire-guard, where Mum aired our clothes while she bathed us in the tin tub.

I can remember fetching the baby's powder from the utility sideboard. What a treasure store that was! Groceries one end, Sunday-best crockery the other, with stockings, suspender-belts, Aspros, insurance books and later, Dad's medal in the drawers in the middle. We kept coal in the cupboard under the stairs, but as there was never enough fuel for two fires, the back kitchen was not so much used as passed through, en route to the outside toilet or the bedrooms.

Mum had the front bedroom, with its double bed (and memories and tears), and matching dressing-table and two-drawer chest. There was no wardrobe. We lived for years without wardrobes or coathangers. Coats hung in layers on doorhooks, and everything else lived in cupboards and drawers.

The small back bedroom had been wallpapered by some earlier and presumably affluent tenant. Over the years the tiny pink flowers on cream ground had become monochrome porridge, and the gold around the honesty leaves had turned black. But in the warm summer evenings, the long rosy rays of the setting sun scanned the Mersey, the docks, the debris, and our lavatory roof, to bring a borrowed colour to our precious wallpaper as we drifted into sleep, me in an iron frame bed, and my new baby brother in my old dropside cot.

Mum, me and David. If our situation made us under-privileged I was not often aware of it, partly because there were so many others like us, and partly because my mother's family was so close and supportive. There were scores of aunts and uncles, and cousins beyond counting, and family get-togethers were frequent, boisterous and quite musical, in a piano-bashing 'all together now' kind of way. 'Doing a Turn' was a regular feature of family singsongs, and I got used to doing my bit when asked, not in any precocious way, but just as a matter of course along with all the others.

Losing my father, and having to compete with a new baby for my mother's attention, did leave me with a basic insecurity that I only recognized in later years. But it didn't seem to affect my ability to entertain others if called upon.

And in fact, losing my father when I was just three actually had some positive benefits that likewise only became apparent later. My memories of my father are all happy ones. I recall him as the one who brought me treats, played with me, took me on outings, cuddled me. I adored my Dad. As a Christian adult I have had no difficulties at all in accommodating the idea of God as my Father. The father-pattern imprinted on my subconscious has no terror, no imperfections, no inadequacies.

Only as my little world started to spread beyond the immediate family did I begin to get a new perspective on my environment. If Mum wasn't working, cleaning for better-off people as my grandmother did, she'd sometimes take us out for picnics. We'd head off, the three of us, the pram loaded with packets of sandwiches and a large bottle of dandelion and burdock.

Inland we went, away from the docks, up past the railway bridge, the shops, the bombed-out matchworks, and the stately library, up over the canal bridge to Hatton Hill Park. Here, behind the council offices, pavements gave way to grass, tram-poles to trees, traffic to birdsong, and we would swing and slide, roll and run, and watch the old men playing bowls.

There were newer houses on Hatton Hill, up beyond the park. After I started school I made friends with children from the Hill, and discovered the luxury world of gardens, bathrooms, hot water taps, and the sheer magic of electricity! Houses with electricity had two tremendous boons as far as I was concerned. Fairy lights at Christmas, and ice-lollies in the summer!

To me, Heaven was a place called Hatton Hill. It even had its own little church, a new brick chapel at the top of the rise, with 'St Paul's' in the stained glass over the door, and shiny light oak furnishings inside.

At the end of an afternoon's sojourn in this celestial territory, I'd hang on to the pram and drag my unwilling feet back to the little war-scarred house that was home, my mind filled with a clear vision of the better life.

We always had prayers at bed-time.

'God bless Mummy and David. God bless Nanny and Grandad. And Aunty Gladys and Uncle John and Pat.'

'And please make Theresa better?'

'And please make Theresa better.'

'And thank you for a sunny day?'

'And thank you for a sunny day.'

'Anything else?'

'No.'

But often I'd be thinking very hard about those who lived on Hatton Hill. Would that be too big a favour to ask?

My grandmother's home was a convenient halfway house between me and my dreams. It was in the same urban district as Hatton Hill, but it fell short of the ultimate distinction by being situated on the wrong side of the canal bridge. When my mother took regular work in a factory, with long hours, David and I were left up here with our beloved Nanny, and we were able to stop and play in the park after school if we wished.

However, a child's early acceptance of the status quo meant that in fact I rarely worried consciously about the 'haves' and 'have nots'. And at Junior School I was far from unhappy. With my best friend Marjorie I even found a much better way of coming home from school than just dawdling in the park. It was far greater fun to dance in the streets!

Away from the main road, in the posh privacy of the quiet back streets where families lived in the back room and kept the front parlour for Sundays, Christmas and laying out, Marj and I became 'The Odeon Sisters'. Our name and our repertoire came from the local cinema where we weekly fell beneath the spell of the great god Hollywood.

Marj was a fantastic Ginger Rogers. Well, she had the hair for it. I was perhaps a rather plump Fred Astaire, but no matter. We'd tippety-tap our way along the deserted side-streets to 'Let's Face the Music and Dance'.

Or she'd be Betty Hutton and I'd be Howard Keel for selections from 'Annie Get Your Gun'. Occasionally, 'Anything You Can Do, I Can Do Better' would get out of hand, and we'd banter, 'No you can't!', 'Yes, I can!' on and on as we played 'tick' round the gateposts of the tiny front gardens.

Musically we were fairly adventurous, for we were both blessed with what they call a good musical ear. We were naturals, who could do instant charabanc harmony to absolutely anything, and did. Even when it wasn't entirely appropriate, like our 'gold and old rose' version of 'God Save The King' on Empire Day. Another favourite technique was for one of us to hold the melody while the other supplied a one-man harpy chorus. We over-played this, too, finding nothing at all funny in 'Me (it's me!) — And (and my!) — My Shad (it's me and my shad!) — Ow!'

Inside school, we were taken in hand by Miss Taylor, who taught us recorder and eurhythmic dance. These were the days before Educational Dance or even Music and Movement. Not for us the joys of free expression in being a tree or a falling leaf. Ours was a more measured pleasure, where the graceful steps and gestures were learned and rehearsed until we had a comprehensive repertoire from which we could compose whole dances. A kind of physical busking. So Marj and I took to it like ducks to water, stripped to knickers and vests, and in winter our liberty bodices!

I loved learning the recorder. I'd have practised every waking hour had it not been so wretchedly unpopular with the rest of the family. David regularly pinched and hid the whistle end, and when we were at Nanny's, music was banished to the wash-house, which put the back kitchen and pantry between my noise and my Grandad, snoozing in his rocker in front of the kitchen range.

But the wash-house turned out to be a lovely studio. The lime-washed walls made it pleasantly light, the resonant acoustic flattered the tone of my bakelite instrument, and the rollers and drip-tray of the iron mangle made an excellent music stand.

We'd practise for hours, Marj and I, and we gradually worked our way up to becoming joint leaders of the school recorder group. Our natural feel for busking together enabled us automatically to match our breathing, phrasing, trills and ornaments with a maturity not often found in junior bands. Soon our school began to achieve distinctions at the local music festivals.

But oh, the dismay that awful year when our official photograph as winners arrived. For there we all were on the little regency dais in our hand-me-down frocks and cardies, Miss Taylor standing proudly stage left, the rest of us posing with our recorders behind our music stands.

I was the big smile in the middle.

At the far end, stage right, from where she had so skilfully led the second descants, was Marj's music stand. And just off the picture was Marj. Or rather, wasn't.

How I laughed! Not at my friend's misfortune, but at the ineptness of the so-called 'professional' photographer!

At ten, I had a lot more to laugh at than to cry about.

Chapter 2

❋ Growing up a Methodist

I became a Methodist by mistake when I was fourteen.

A friend at school asked me to go with her to a club one evening, and I thought she meant the table-tennis club where her father was secretary and coach. She didn't, though. She meant the girls' club at her church, and by the time I realized I wasn't going to be groomed for selection for the English table-tennis team I was having such a good time it didn't matter.

We were taught gymnastics and judo by Mr Bennett, an ex-army PE instructor, and crafts and handwork by Miss Rostock. In overall charge was Miss Baker, who also led a girls' Bible class on a different evening.

I hadn't met anyone quite like Miss Baker. She was pretty, but not young, and the girls told me that her fiancé had died on the eve of their wedding. The bridal gown in the dressing-up box was actually hers, they said. The pathos rang bells with me and I loved her from the start.

She was a very lovable person anyway. We knew she went to work, but she did also seem to be something of a millionairess. In winter she came to the club in a taxi, calling it back later to take us all home in fours and fives, and every member's birthday was celebrated with trays of cream cakes borne into the church hall by the regular cab-driver-cum-Jeeves.

But it wasn't just these touches of luxury that won us. Miss Baker had something about her personality that was fascinating. She could be quite scatterbrained, losing our half-finished craft projects and immediately buying new ones. She could be strict, insisting that we cleared away the oil-paints and the teacups in time for the Epilogue each week. But no matter how surly or stubborn or thoroughly unreliable we might be in these stormy teen years, I never once saw her discouraged or cross.

At the Bible class, which I soon joined, she bought us all Bibles and note-books, and worked through the Gospels, telling us about Jesus in a way I found both compelling and shocking. She spoke of him as if she knew him personally!

At the end of the lesson came the part I liked best. Miss Baker would dictate to us seven different verses selected from the Bible, one for each day of the following week, and we'd write them down carefully in our notebooks. Our task then was to locate the references for each passage. We none of us had any knowledge of such aids as Bible dictionaries or concordances. We just spent our spare time thumbing through our Bibles, trying to recognize passages which seemed to be 'in tune' with the day's verse. It amazes me now to think that most of us would find most of the verses each week. But it endowed me with a tremendous 'feel' for what comes where in the Bible, for which I'm still constantly grateful.

I'd been baptized in the Church of England as a baby, but my mother didn't often go to church, and David and I had been sent to Sunday school only sporadically. So there were no problems of 'changing' or disloyalty when I became accepted as an adult member in the Methodist church at sixteen and was put under Miss Baker's further supervision. The Wesleyan class system was still a strong feature of this particular church, with all the adult members meeting regularly with their class leaders for moral and spiritual support.

Miss Baker found ways of supporting 'her girls' that went far beyond the call of duty. Having noticed my keen interest in music, she asked if I were having lessons of any sort.

I explained that I'd been given an old piano but my mother couldn't afford to send me to a teacher. Miss Baker probably knew all this anyway, but she came up with what seemed like an original suggestion. If the church paid for me to have lessons, would my mother allow me to be the Sunday school pianist?

My mother was well-practised at accepting other people's kindnesses with grace and genuine appreciation, so I was introduced to a local concert pianist and teacher who gladly took me as a pupil, and sent his bills in due course not to the church *per se* but to Miss Baker herself.

In the next couple of years I became a very good Sunday school pianist, which pleased everyone except my teacher. He recognized my general musicianship and was very frustrated to find it just would not be moulded into concert performances. I could play any hymn in the book, in any key, and I could busk any hymn not in the book, or any tune from the 'top twenty', for that matter. (I learned to call this particular facility 'keyboard harmony' at examination time!) But when it came to Bach preludes and fugues, the Beethoven sonatas and the Mendelssohn 'Songs without Words', my dear teacher could not push me further than Grade Six.

To some extent I shared his frustration. Music was my favourite subject at school. I even cherished hopes of becoming a school music teacher myself one day. But I was obviously not a 'natural' pianist. And I was certainly not a concert pianist! Maybe I was studying the wrong instrument.

We had at home a very old Spanish guitar once played by my father. I retrieved it from the 'glory hole' above the stair-well in the back bedroom and dusted it down. All the strings were broken, so I scoured the house for replacements, eventually pinching several yards of mackerel line from David's fishing tackle. But I'd no idea which notes the strings should be tuned to play.

Suddenly I remembered the little symbols printed above the piano parts on the hundreds of old sheet music songs I found irresistible at jumble sales. On closer inspection, they turned out to be drawings of where to put your fingers to make the chords on a ukelele, and which notes to tune the four strings to.

I realized that the guitar ought really to have six strings, even if they're only fishing line, but I was undeterred. On four strings only, I was soon conversant with enough ukelele chords to accompany all the hits of the years between the wars. But there had to be serious doubts as to whether this particular musical activity would enhance my chances of getting into teacher training college! And once I was in the sixth form, getting into college to study music was the one goal I was aiming for.

'Look,' said my piano teacher, disguising his growing despair with a positive attack, 'why don't you join the Merseyside Youth Orchestra?'

'I can't do that! I don't play a proper orchestral instrument!'

'I didn't mean as a player, exactly', he went on. 'Why don't you see if they'll just let you sit in on rehearsals? You'd learn a lot of standard works from the inside, so to speak. You know, symphony structure, orchestration, things like that. Then at least you could talk like a musician at your college interview. It would do you no harm, anyway. Give it a try.'

So I did. And some remarkable things happened in quick succession.

First of all, Mr Jenkins, the Youth Orchestra's conductor, wouldn't hear of me not playing. I served a three-week apprenticeship on the triangle, during which time I learned how to read an orchestral part and count, accurately, the necessary bars' rest before entries.

Then he produced an old brass tuba and announced: 'You'd be a lot more use to us if you could play this thing. See if John can show you the rudiments.'

And he sent me off, with the unwieldy instrument under my arm, to find John Courtie, the orchestra's first trumpet and leader of the whole brass section.

That first day on the tuba I learned to play one very basic scale, changing the valves and the lip-pressure, and on the strength of this small achievement I applied to Bretton Hall training college as a potential music student, first study piano, second study tuba. And I was accepted. But before I took my place at college, I'd fallen for my tuba tutor at the Youth Orchestra.

'Tell me about this new boyfriend, then', said Miss Baker as she wheeled the laden tea-trolley into the sitting-room. She regularly invited us, 'her girls', to come individually to have tea at her house so that we could talk things through with her if we wanted to.

'The one who plays the trumpet', she said. 'What's his name? John?'

'Yes. That's right.'

I sighed and pulled a face.

'Oh, I don't know. He's a puzzle. Can't make him out at all.'

'How do you mean, dear?'

'Well, for a start, he's much cleverer than me. He's going to Oxford, you know. And this is the first time I've had a boyfriend cleverer than me. I'm not sure I like it!'

'If you ask me,' said my counsellor as I tucked into a doughnut, 'that's a very good thing.'

I licked the sugar from my lips and asked her, 'Why do you say that?'

She looked at me carefully, smiling as she selected her words.

'I reckon you're old enough now not to need to have your ego bolstered.'

'Sorry,' I said, blushing a little. 'I'm not with you.'

'Think about it. All your other boyfriends could have been chosen specially to make you feel superior in some way. Attractive, or intellectual, or amusing.'

Faces from the church boys' club presented themselves accusingly.

'It wasn't like that at all!' I protested. 'They were nice! I liked them!'

'Of course you did, dear', said Miss Baker gently, 'But at the same time, there was no real risk of you being rejected by any of them. Who usually called things off when ardours cooled?'

'Well, now you ask, me, I think.'

'Exactly. A little girl whose world was once turned topsy-turvy by circumstances beyond her control, is quite likely to make relationships later where she's absolutely sure she's holding the reins.'

I drank my tea in silence. It was a completely new thought. But it made a lot of sense.

After a while I said: 'I see now why I've been rattled. I mean, I know I like *him*, but I don't like the . . . er,' I struggled to find words to express my dilemma, 'well, the balance between us, I suppose. He calls the tune, a lot of the time, and I'm not used to it.'

'My dear, if you can take it, I'm sure you'll be the better for it', said Miss Baker as she cut me a piece of fruit cake. 'Exposing old wounds to the risk of a knock or two is the best way of making sure they heal. It takes time, of course.'

God bless her, I thought. She'd know a great deal about old hurts.

'Anyway,' she said cheerfully, 'when do we get to meet this lion-tamer?'

I laughed uneasily. 'Er, that's another thing, actually. He's not at all religious. There's no way I can get him to church.'

'Oh, I don't know,' she said. 'It's early days yet. Best if you don't push it, I think. He may feel threatened himself for all we know.'

Goodness! What an idea! But again, it made sense.

Miss Baker made a lot of sense.

I know now that she also prayed a lot of prayers.

Somehow John and I made the balance work in a way that

suited the two of us, and by the time we both left Liverpool, me for Yorkshire, him for Oxford, we knew we wanted to be married when we finally came back.

Chapter 3

❋ Jazz and Jesus

We called it a 'teacher training college', but Bretton Hall seemed intent on resisting the label.

The grand eighteenth-century house sat proudly astride its palladian portico at the centre of three hundred acres of parkland beneath High Hoyland, determined to stay faithful to its Capability Brown landscapes and lakes. Maybe the newer residents could be charmed into believing they were perhaps guests at a longish country house-party?

Certainly, as the students were pursuing music, art and drama as their main subjects, the pretence was not difficult. The Hall's elegant interiors were constantly enhanced by music and madrigals, sculptures and paintings inspired by the woodlands, or the performing of some local mystery plays, older than Bretton itself. Teachers of the future, we savoured the past, taking breakfast in the Adam dining-room, reading in the old library, painting in the orangery and even dressing for dinner.

The vast bedrooms around the main upstairs landing were named after different parts of the estate, and I was allotted to 'Bentley Springs' with two Barbaras, a Christine and a Gill. By day the tall window near my bed looked out over the terrace garden, the upper lake and the deer park (with its Bentley Springs). By night, it let in sounds of the countryside, wind in the trees, animals in the undergrowth, while I lay awake missing the buses, the drunks and the ships' hooters on the Mersey!

This complete change of life-style was far too fascinating for me to be homesick. For example, my mother's widowed status ensured me a maximum government grant. So here in my new stately home, I found myself with access not only to more money than I'd ever been used to before, but more even than some fellow-students were getting from their mill-owner fathers. I sent my mother cash at regular intervals and blossoms from the camellia house each spring.

The living was not quite so gracious in the cellar practice-rooms, however. Although there was a discreet new block of airy practice-rooms with pianos at the back of the house, 'other instruments' were banished to the nether regions, an underground warren of fluorescent-lit cells linked by echoing alleys.

Encouraged by Mr Bradshaw, the brass tutor, who decided early on that I had the makings of a fair tuba-player, I spent a lot of my time 'below stairs'. Relaxing in the peculiar solitude of a solo instrument trapped by sound-proofed walls, I worked at my 'Twelve Russian Studies', until they came to an abrupt halt one evening when the door burst open and my sanctuary was invaded by two bearded young men.

'There! I told you there was another one!'

'But she's a girl!'

'Of course she's a girl! What difference does it make? Is that or is that not a tuba?'

'Right. That is certainly a tuba.'

It was a tuba of sorts. I'd handed back the Youth Orchestra instrument to Mr Jenkins and was now learning on a college instrument that had seen better days. It was badly dented, the leaky water-key was fastened shut with knotted red string, and three of the metal stays had come adrift and had been somewhat inadequately reinforced with sticky tape.

'I'm sorry,' I said, 'is there some bother about me having this? Mr Bradshaw said I could use it as my own.'

'And you're more than welcome, I should say!'

I'd already pinned him as a Welshman before his colleague announced: 'Idris has his own wotsit, er, tuba. Trouble is, we need him to play trombone in the band.'

I hadn't seen either of these characters in the college

wind band, that loud and lively siding where I'd been shunted along with all the other brass and wind players not good enough for the college orchestra.

So I asked, 'What band?'

'Why, the Jazz Band, of course!' said the Welshman. Only, the way he said it, it sounded like Jass Band. Very authentic. Early New Orleans.

'Can you play Dixieland on that thing?' demanded his friend.

'I don't know', I answered with patent honesty, 'How does it go?'

When they'd finished laughing, the Welshman looked at the first of the 'Twelve Russian Studies' and exclaimed, 'Hell, Mike! If she can get round this lot in three weeks, she won't have any trouble with "Tin Roof Blues".'

'Right, then', said Mike, 'You're in!'

'In what?'

They answered in chorus. 'The Jazz Band!'

'But I've never played jazz!' I protested.

'That's what they all say!' laughed Mike.

As they left, Idris said: 'It's a giggle, love, honest. Large practice-room, piano block, eight o'clock tomorrow night. Tata!'

It is absolutely impossible to slip unnoticed into a room whilst carrying a battered old tuba that has a propensity for dropping bits with the capriciousness of a rattle-throwing baby. My entrance was greeted with loud cheers from the rest of the band, and Idris quickly did the introductions.

'Jim Clifton on piano, Drama and English. Paul, er, Thomson wasn't it? Yes, Paul Thomson on clarinet. He's a first-year musician like yourself.' I recognized the first clarinettist from the wind band.

'Mike Edwards on trumpet you've already met, English and Art. I'm going onto trombone now you're here, but I'm really the college's other tuba-player, Idris Price. Gentlemen, this is, er, Brenda. Right?'

'Right. I hope you told them I'm new to all this?'

'The way we play, love, you could do your Russian Studies and no one would notice!'

Jim stubbed out a cigarette in the ash-tray on top of the piano. 'Still no drums, Idris?'

'There's a first-year potter who's keen, but he can't count. I felt we had to draw the line of incompetence slightly above that!'

'Right then. Let's see how we do with "Darktown Strutter's Ball" for starters.'

When Jim swung into a tinkling intro with heavy bass, a thousand memories flooded back, of family 'do's' with Aunty Kath at the piano. Then as I watched the others blend into the first chorus together, another familiarity asserted itself. I'd done this before, surely? With Marj? Yes, of course! They were busking!

Oh, they paid allegiance to a common chord progression, a 'reference' melody and Jim's authoritative left hand. But within this framework they improvised freely.

I crept in on the second chorus, and found my way through the sequence as quietly as possible. For the third and final chorus, I opened up and 'oompahed' briskly round the appropriate bass-scales with some exhilaration.

After the 'Hi-tiddly-eye-tye, brown bread!' ending, they swooped on me.

'I thought you said you couldn't play?'

'Where did you learn to do that?'

'That was no Russian Study, now. Be honest!'

It's a truism in the music world that the professionals are the professionals because they play for their living. Meaning that if you can afford to spend all your time playing your musical instrument, you're bound to get good!

The improvement in my general tuba-playing during my time at Bretton Hall was in part due to the fact that I spent many hours playing it. And much of that time was with the Jazz Band. Traditional jazz became a hobby that paid dividends in agility and stamina for the Russian Studies and their like.

Tuba apart, I was hardly likely to make my mark on the college. I was miles behind the other first-study pianists and even more of a trial to my college piano tutor than I had been to my teacher in Liverpool. The compulsory psychology lectures were a hostile jungle of long words and strange secrets. And the only time I shone in compulsory English was when the lecturer set us to write four lines of iambic tetrameters against a stop-watch. I produced:

> *The moose ran loose on yonder hill*
> *And trod upon the daffodil.*
> *It ran amok among the trees*
> *And wore its feet down to its knees.*

> in less than ten seconds.

Worse than any academic struggles were the emotional wrestling bouts I seemed constantly to be locked in.

I was committed to John, but attracted to Idris.

I was immature and teetotal, but the only place to go out in the evenings was the pub in the next village.

I was a God-fearing Methodist, but unable to articulate my beliefs to my sophisticated atheist peers. Totally unused as I was to any kind of heated debate, the cliché-ridden arguments that ricocheted round the common-room long after we got back from the pub left me feeling chastised and weepy.

Halfway through my first year at Bretton, a chance misunderstanding led to me being torn off a strip by a fearsome lady psychology lecturer. That night I had the most awful nightmare, and was shaken awake by my room-mates who'd been alarmed by my screams.

I'd never had nightmares before. If that was what this rarified arty existence was doing to me, I knew better than to stick around. Next morning, when the other first-years filed into the lecture-room, I caught the village bus to the nearest town and main-line railway station. I was going home.

Or so I thought.

But one of the Barbaras had alerted the vice-principal, and just as the train drew in, I felt her gently take my arm.

It was no dramatic return to college. I'd only been gone for a morning and few people had missed me. But Jacquie did. She sought me out later, made me a coffee and let me ramble on at her.

'Jacquie,' I said, 'doesn't it bother you, all this "there's no such thing as God" and "every man his own moral governor" business? I mean, you're a . . . what it is? A Baptist? They believe in God, don't they?'

'I should hope so!' she laughed.

'But how is it these liberal ideas don't rattle you like they do me? How can you bear to live among such atheistic people?'

'You're beginning to sound like an Old Testament prophet', she said, 'but I'll tell you. The thing is, Brenda, they can dispute till they're blue in the face, but none of their arguments is a match for my own experience. They can say there's no God, but I have a day-by-day relationship with him. To them, he's a topic for debate. To me he's a real and powerful person. I try to put a word in here and there, but I don't have to prove God's existence to myself by scoring points off the others. D'you follow?'

'Mmm. I think so.'

Jacquie lived across the landing from me and we saw each other often enough in music lectures and the like for me to think of her as a friend. But I was beginning to see that I hadn't really known her very well at all. I knew she was a churchgoer. Sometimes she'd been with me to the Methodist chapel in the village because there wasn't a local Baptist church. But I hadn't realized that her quiet unruffled approach to life was not just one of those psychological traits I'd been learning about. Suddenly, a penny dropped. If it wasn't just a matter of personality, then I could perhaps get to where Jacquie was?

I said, carefully: 'Jacquie. I know I believe in God, and I

do read my Bible and pray to him. But I couldn't really say I had a close relationship with him, like you seem to.'

As I hesitated over my next words, she answered: 'Oh, you're in very good company. Think of old Nicodemus.'

'Old Nick *who?*'

'You know. The Pharisee in John's Gospel. He was religious, moral, well-educated, but he still felt he was missing out on something.'

'Yes.' I remembered the incident. 'He went to see Jesus by night.'

For the first time, a familiar Bible story took on a new relevance as I sieved through it for a personal message for me.

Jacquie picked up the Bible from my bedside table.

'Do you remember what Jesus told him? Look, here in chapter three. "You must be born again".'

'I never really understood what that meant,' I confessed.

'Neither did Nicodemus!' was Jacquie's answer. 'But if you read through the New Testament, you see it happening to lots of people. They admit they're dissatisfied with themselves, they accept that Jesus died as a kind of penalty for their selfish independence — sin, the Bible calls it. And they hand over their life to him in gratitude. And that point where they turn away from the old life and put themselves "under new management", well, that's just like a new birth.'

'Yes, but how does that give you a close relationship with God? I mean, you seem to know him, personally.'

I remembered Miss Baker. More pennies were dropping.

'Well, once you decide to go in for this "under new management" scheme, you find God has moved in. You become aware of his Spirit, not just with you but in you. You find him easy to approach in prayer, and you feel him nudging you into the ways he wants you to go.'

'It seems to work for you,' I said.

'It could for you, too,' she replied.

I suppose Jacquie must have realized I needed time on my

own to think. Maybe the Spirit nudged her and told her to back off. Anyway, she picked up the coffee mugs and crossed to the door.

'I'll just wash these, then I must have another look at this week's harmony assignment. And by the way . . .'

She paused with just her head cocked round the door to say: 'Nicodemus must have decided it made sense. When Joseph of Arimathea provided a tomb for Jesus, it was "old Nick" who supplied the embalming spices. Obviously thought a lot of his new manager. 'Bye.'

There was a tiny chapel in the college cellar, far enough away from the practice-rooms to be called the 'Quiet Room'. Some days later I knelt alone before the plain altar-table and prayed a very simple prayer. I asked God's forgiveness for trying to manage my own life, thanked Jesus for taking my punishment, and asked the Holy Spirit to come into my life as the 'new manager'.

Call it conversion, call it growing up, but from that point I settled into life generally with a new sense of purpose and a new sense of identity. The rising panic of deep-seated insecurity gradually succumbed more and more to the assurance that God was actually in control of my life. There were still conflicts, but nothing I couldn't handle with an honest approach to God in prayer. I learned from Jacquie, who prayed with me every evening for several weeks, that praying is talking to God, honestly, 'cards on the table'.

She and the other members of the tiny college Christian Fellowship doubtless made an irradicable impression on me when it came to 'being a Christian'. They weren't at all po-faced 'Holy Joes', but they did take the Bible seriously. If it said it, one did it!

They didn't criticize my activities with the Jazz Band. In fact, they tended to see it as something of a public relations opportunity within the college. But some of the places I found myself playing with the band outside college raised the odd eyebrow.

I remember one Barnsley pub, famous for its live entertainment, where we were slotted in the bill between a Scottish piper and a strip-tease artiste. The Scotsman needed no extra accompaniment, but the stripper handed us band-parts for her music, the theme tune from the old TV series 'Rawhide'!

In the audience that night was the manager of a nearby night-club. At closing time, he came bounding up on to the platform looking for 'the lass who played euphonium and sang "Shimmy like my Sister Kate"'.

That was me.

He'd already signed up the 'other' stripper, he said, but what he really wanted was some unique new attraction for his club. Now, a young lady in a bowler hat and bow tie (he didn't mention my very modest pink gingham dress), who would do the 'Shimmy' and play the, er . . . 'What d'yer call it?'

'Tuba, but I . . .'

'Yes, the tuba. Eh, now that'd be something! What d'you say?'

I said I was flattered by his interest, but that I was appearing under false pretences. I wasn't a bona fide entertainer, I was a serious music student.

'But thank you for asking!'

Then I fled to the Ladies'!

John's attitude to religion was that it was something you pursued only if you felt the need. Obviously I felt the need, he admitted, as we talked about it one weekend when he came to visit me at Bretton. But as he was perfectly happy with himself and his life without religion, would I do him a favour and stop pestering him!

This difference between us worried me more than it worried him. I took the Bible's warning against being 'unequally yoked' very seriously. I could see the difficulties faced by any married couple whose basic philosophies were so divergent. I did stop pestering but I didn't stop praying.

The Christian Fellowship had John at the top of their 'intercessions' list for months and never moaned or lost heart.

It was some time in my second year that I got the letter from Oxford describing John's conversion. Someone had taken him to hear a lecture by Maurice Wood, who later became Bishop of Norwich. I can only suppose that it took another 'academic' to adequately pin-point John's need for God in appropriate terms. Certainly, he made a complete about-turn and gave his life to the Lord that same evening.

When I'd read his letter three times to assure myself I hadn't imagined what it said, I went screaming off for Jacquie and we danced and sang our praises, deaf to the patronizing 'tuts' of our uncomprehending colleagues.

After three years at Bretton Hall, I returned to Liverpool a qualified teacher, having passed my final music examinations as a fairly competent tuba-player and a more than adequate pianist, in that order. I think the tuba was God-given; I could never have qualified with piano as my first instrument.

Mr Jenkins, who had first handed me the tuba at the Youth Orchestra, was pleased to welcome me back. As music adviser for the Liverpool Education Committee he appointed me to a Roman Catholic girls' school not far from my home.

I loved my job. The pupils were a rough and ready lot, but great fun. There were minor skirmishes, such as the time young Kathleen tried to finish her illegal break-time cigarette behind her desklid and set fire to all her books! But we learned sonata form by analyzing the Beatles' hits and sight-singing by a kind of home-brew semaphore, and there were seldom any truants from music lessons.

There were touching moments, too. A local hero was Michael Holliday, the popular ballad-singer, and the community was shocked when he committed suicide. When the funeral cortège crept past the school in the early morning before I'd finished calling the class register, the girls left their desks in silence and stood at the windows, crossing themselves and mouthing tearful prayers.

My own church activities had undergone a fairly dramatic transformation. The Methodist church I'd known before college had closed down, and its members were travelling to another Methodist church much further from my home. For a while I attended an Anglican church near the Gladstone Dock, but just as I was beginning to feel at home there, the vicar asked me if I would consider helping out at the daughter church, where they needed a pianist.

Once I was settled in at this church, St Mary's, fully integrated into its life and worship, it seemed logical to ask about confirmation. My thinking coincided with John's. He was still at Oxford worshipping at St Ebbe's, but he decided to postpone his confirmation until he was back in Liverpool.

At the end of John's course, we were married in St Mary's by the whizz-kid curate, a former gas-fitter whose down-to-earth faith taught us a lot.

'Prayers have legs,' he'd say, 'and they're usually your own!'

Another helper in the parish was Dave, a young public school ordinand from the south whose bishop had sent him to Bootle for a year between university and theological college to 'see how the other half lives'. He had ample opportunity, working as a progress-chaser at Plessey's by day, and as parish assistant evenings and weekends.

Dave was sometimes exhausted, often bewildered, but he never once doubted his call. Indeed, he became enthusiastically determined to minister in Liverpool eventually, and he couldn't help infecting others with his enthusiasm.

'You ought at least to consider the full-time ministry,' he said to John, soon after our marriage.

'I'll think about it,' John promised.

I don't suppose either of us expected it to come to anything. But the seed was sown. We were thinking about it.

Chapter 4

✳ Toxteth to Oxfordshire

Everyone knows Toxteth since the summer riots of 1981. But when John and I moved there after our marriage, the ancient name that once encompassed a vast hunting forest had all but fallen into disuse. If you lived in Toxteth then, you called it 'Liverpool 8'; its postal number. Everyone did.

In the late 'swinging sixties', when Liverpool 8 was synonymous with the offbeat culture that swelled to accompany the music of the Merseybeat era, one of the newspaper magazines did a feature on the character, and characters, of the area.

Stark black and white photographs captured the flaking stucco of the Georgian terrace houses, mostly let as flats or bedsits, where the colourful artists and poets lived. Poets like Roger McGough and Adrian Henri, whose laugh-or-cry verses sang their Scouse metres to the world. Artists like Arthur Dooley, the ex-docker sculpting in metal to fuse Catholicism and Communism. And musician Fritz Spiegl, then principal flautist with the Royal Liverpool Philarmonic Orchestra, but noted more for his theme tune for the TV series 'Z-Cars'. Six glossy pages celebrated Liverpool 8 and never once called it Toxteth!

In our own crumbling Georgian terrace facing Prince's Park, the 'no children' rule meant we were mostly early marrieds or singles. But the streets to the back of the house were rather less disciplined, and echoed with the noisy games of children of all colours, West Indian 'Patricks' and Chinese 'Billys' among them.

Toxteth, whilst bordering the Mersey like Bootle, is several miles further south on the other side of the city, which made keeping in touch with St Mary's a bit difficult. John and I commuted for a while, but soon we began to feel we ought to be committed to a local church.

But which church? Toxteth was littered with churches of every description, from the quaint seventeenth-century Unitarian chapel to the enormous Baptist Tabernacle, 'Tocky Tab' to the locals.

We prayed for guidance as to where to worship, and almost immediately came upon a newspaper article about a Toxteth vicar looking for help with his youth work. Off we went to see him, and he invited us to throw in our lot with his small congregation at St Bede's, and particularly to nurture the little group of young people who gathered after the Sunday evening service.

Only after everything was settled did we learn from John's parents that they had been married at this same St Bede's, and that John was baptized there as a baby. So it seemed quite fitting for him to welcome these youngsters into our flat each Sunday, when we'd sing together to his guitar, drink gallons of coffee, and study the Bible with them.

One day our vicar asked John: 'What did you read for your degree?'

'French.'

'And what exactly are you doing now?'

'Management training with Selfridge's.'

'Have you ever considered the full-time ministry?'

There it was again!

This time we felt obliged not merely to think about it, but to pray about it, seriously.

The answer came quite quickly.

John was invited to return to Oxford to research some medieval literature for a doctor's degree.

'What do you think?' I asked him.

'I think I'd like to do it.'

'Where are you up to on the ministry question?'

'No problem, really', John assured me with a smile, 'I can

only do the research if I get a major state studentship. They're pretty scarce, so if I don't get one, then it's obviously "no" to the research and we push the door marked "ministry".'

That sounded fair enough, I thought.

But by the time we'd heard that John had been awarded his studentship, we had something else to weave into our planning. I was pregnant, and the baby was due to arrive some three months before the start of John's new studies.

Fortunately, our landlord was very understanding, as were the other tenants in our house. In fact, because of the 'no children' rule, our son Gavin's arrival was a novelty that generated a good deal of fuss. We were showered with gifts, and the two deaconesses from 'Tocky Tab', who lived in the top flat, came down to film 'mother and baby' with their new home-movie outfit.

A few weeks after Gavin's baptism at St Bede's, we said goodbye to Toxteth, and to Bootle, and pointed our recently acquired but very ancient Ford Popular towards Royal Berkshire.

We'd have preferred to be heading for Oxford itself, but the rents there were far beyond our means. Instead, our destination was to be a large but cheap flat above a shop in a small town, nineteen miles south-west of the university city.

John knew I was disappointed. I'd so looked forward to pushing the pram to St Ebbe's or St Aldate's, to hear the really 'big name' speakers of the day.

'Don't worry, darling,' he comforted as we rumbled our way south, 'I'm sure we'll all love Faringdon. Just you see.'

As we approached it from the north, Faringdon gave no hint of existence, no distant display of olde worlde charm, other than the Folly Tower that topped the wooded hill on its eastern edge. Even the manor, Faringdon House, could hide completely behind the massive trees in those days before Dutch elm disease.

With no chance to focus in gradually, I had to be ready

for anything. Suddenly the country road met a T-junction on a ridge and we were confronted by a row of tall houses adjoining each other but every one of them different. John spotted the squat church down to the right, and two turns later we were in the centre of a busy 'crossroads' town, with traffic growling through between Oxford and Swindon, Wantage and Cirencester.

We circled the strange old Cotswold building stuck up on pillars in the centre of the Market Place, and pulled up opposite the Corn Exchange.

'Here we are.' John leaned across me to check the name of the grocer's shop where we'd stopped. 'That's the door to our flat. As soon as I've got you and the baby safely inside, I'll have to move the car.'

'Why?' I asked him. 'I mean, we live here, don't we?'

'Yes, but just look! It's a busy trunk road. See, yellow lines!'

That was my first illusion shattered. Life at the centre of a 'quiet' country town was going to be very much noisier than in our city flat in a sleepy parkside road.

Faringdon's next surprise was its size. Or lack of it. On our second afternoon we went out exploring and crossed the town from end to end. Back home, I checked our maps. Our new town could be slotted into one of Liverpool's big city parks!

But Faringdon was undeniably pretty. Although it was still in Berkshire (local government reorganization later placed it in Oxfordshire), John Betjeman called it the southernmost tip of the Oxfordshire Cotswolds because of the uniform use of the regional stone. The town lay in the Vale of the White Horse, between the Downs to the south, with the famous 'horse' up above Uffington, and the Thames to the north, with Lechlade's 'first lock'. Its strategic position at the convergence of several ancient roads was reflected in the great number of inns we came across on our walk. Thirteen hostelries for a population of less than four thousand!

We found four churches dotted around the centre. Apart from the ivy-clad Norman parish church, there was a historic old Baptist chapel, an eighteenth-century Congregational church, and a nineteenth-century Methodist church. It seemed as if ecumenism had been creeping in slowly for hundreds of years. While the baby cooed from his pram, we made a note of the times of services from the four notice-boards. We fully expected to join the Anglican church, but were nonetheless prepared to keep one ear cocked for any contrary instruction from the Holy Spirit.

As we jotted down the details from the Methodist board, a voice behind us said, 'You thinking of joining us, then?'

The stocky young man with rosy cheeks and ready smile was Ian, a Methodist local preacher, we learned as we exchanged introductions. He assured us of a warm welcome from the Anglicans, but for all that still invited us to his own home for our first Sunday evening, to meet his wife Shirley.

Ian was right about the Anglican welcome. After the morning service, the vicar and his wife ('Please call us Edmund and Gwen') took us to the vicarage for coffee and introduced us to the new curate and his wife.

'Terry and Jill are new here, like yourselves. I dare say you'll find you've plenty in common.'

The next morning another couple rang our doorbell as they took a break from their shopping. The rather serious young man was Bill, student pastor of the Baptist chapel. The girl with him was Anthea, his wife. Edmund had told Bill of John's arrival, and suggested that the two students might share the travelling to Oxford.

So within a week we'd made eight friends, four Anglicans, two Methodists and two Baptists. And we'd discovered that our flat was just the place for them to stop for coffee while doing their shopping!

To complete the ecumenical circle, our nearest neighbours were the Congregational minister and his wife, whose church and manse were next-door-but-one to 'our' shop.

Perhaps because of our very central flat, we were soon introducing friends to friends across the denominations, despite being newcomers ourselves. The ministers of the town's churches were happy to see links developing between their respective 'flocks', because they themselves were friends who met regularly to pray and support each other in their work.

John very quickly became happily immersed in his research, and I joined the Young Wives at the parish church and helped Jill with the children's 'Pathfinder' group. Sometimes John and I sang together, with his guitar, at Pathfinder services, and Edmund wasn't slow in booking us for his Harvest supper. We sang Liverpool folk-songs (a novelty after the Beatles), and laughingly refused the proffered fee at the end of the evening.

Meanwhile, some of Bill's youngsters from the Baptist chapel had taken to gathering at our flat on Sunday evenings, with his full approval. Their Berkshire burr with touches of Wiltshire west-country was very different from the Scouse twang of our Toxteth teenagers. But their challenges were the same.

'The church is out of date!'

'What's wrong with trial marriage?'

'The ouija board's only a bit of a laugh!'

Again, it was gallons of coffee and 'Let's see what the Bible says about it.'

After a while, we received an invitation to visit one of the Baptist deacons. The youngsters told us: 'Len thinks Bill's off 'is 'ead lettin' us come to your flat!'

Len laughed like a drain when we told him. 'Little horrors!' he chuckled, 'I said no such thing!' And he welcomed us into his comfortable lounge, while Barbara made us tea, and their three little girls mothered their own baby brother and our Gavin in turns.

'Of course, Len,' John began, 'I can quite understand your misgivings . . .'

A blue-eyed moppet with copper curls pushed her dolly's

pram to John's chair.

'Look,' she said proudly, 'twins!'

Her big sisters quickly rescued both babies and Len said: 'Now, please don't get me wrong. I'm delighted with the teaching you're giving our youngsters. And it does help Bill in preparing them for adult baptism. It's just that . . .'

Barbara finished for him, shyly: 'You see, we don't know many Anglicans.'

'Come off it, Barb', Len protested. 'We don't know any Anglicans. Well, only the vicar. Vaguely. Nice bloke.'

'Well,' said John, 'here we are. Only one head apiece, despite all you've heard!'

Having been gently probed about our personal faith during our first visit to our Methodist friends, Ian and Shirley, we could anticipate a Baptist deacon's suspicions. Apparently, some conservative free churches really believed that Anglicans were a breed of empty-headed ritualists, always to be pitied and unlikely to be converted!

But Len and Barbara were better disposed towards us than we might have hoped for, simply because they had themselves courted family disapproval on their arrival in Faringdon, by leaving their strict Brethren background and joining the Baptists. They knew what it felt like to be 'beyond the pale'. Of all our new friends we identified most readily with them and, in time, came to look on them as our older brother and sister 'in the Lord'.

Despite having lived in the same road as Ian and Shirley for two years, Len and Barbara didn't actually know them, beyond the occasional 'good morning'. Amazed, we rectified this immediately by doing our now familiar act of introducing denomination to denomination. And about the same time, Edmund invited John, Ian and Len (and wives when available) to serve on a new inter-denominational evangelistic committee, to foster non-church activities that would bring the gospel to more of the town's non-churchgoers. He threw us in at the deep end, organizing the hiring of buses to the Oxford relay of Billy Graham's 'All-Britain' crusade, and making friends with the townspeople who filled them.

Ian and I were acting as counsellors at the Oxford meetings, where we were supervised by a small, stern lady who gave the impression that a sense of humour was a distinct disadvantage to any Christian. She also guarded the special literature like the Keeper of the Crown Jewels. Every last leaflet had to be accounted for and some return reported (e.g. a converted enquirer) for each missing piece.

One evening, Ian asked if he might take home one conselling envelope, which contained a Gospel of John and the first lesson in a postal Bible study course. Our supervisor lectured him severely on the cost of these items and the potential catastrophic waste if every counsellor should lose just one envelope, but finally allowed Ian to put the packet in his pocket only after he promised her faithfully that there was someone on our bus who would quite definitely be converted on the way home.

Outside the hall Ian stopped to examine the envelope carefully.

'What are you looking for?' I asked.

'Her long piece of elastic', he replied without a hint of a smile.

Inside the bus, Ian sat next to a workmate whose wife had recently become a committed Christian in response to a sermon from Edmund. Before we reached Faringdon, Ian called me over to their seat.

'This is Tony', he said. 'I think you've probably met his wife Bobbie.'

'Yes,' I said, 'we're friends at the Young Wives. Hello, Tony. Pleased to meet you.'

Ian looked at me and beamed with all kinds of delight and relief as he announced: 'Tony's just asked God to take over his life.'

In case I hadn't understood, Tony himself said: 'I'm a new committed Christian. I've just been converted.'

Thinking of our supervisor who would be drumming her fingers the next evening waiting for Ian's counselling envelope, I said a heartfelt 'Praise the Lord!'

Tony and Bobbie were so enthusiastic about their new-found faith that Edmund soon co-opted them onto his evangelistic committee. Together we organized lectures and film-shows, coffee mornings and picnics, and under the curate's leadership we opened a youth club in an old hayloft at the back of a town-centre inn, the Red Lion. At the Lion Cub Coffee Club, teenagers who steered clear of church and were an under-age nuisance to the various pub landlords, gathered to hear Christian beat groups, guest evangelists and testimonies from other youngsters with a lively experience of the Lord Jesus.

As we worked and prayed together through all these projects, the eight of us grew closer together as friends — Ian and Shirley, Len and Barbara, Tony and Bobbie and ourselves. We shared meals whenever we could, and got used to praying to the accompaniment of the games of nine or ten children! We even took our holidays together, usually joined by other friends too, filling an entire house of holiday flatlets near Studland Bay. So happy was I in the company of these people, it was painful to recall how unwilling I'd been to come and live amongst them in the first place.

The only cloud, a very small one as it turned out, rolled in at the end of our first year in Faringdon. Our car died of extreme old age. This wouldn't have mattered much, except that our very tight budget depended on cheap motoring for John, in and out of Oxford. Petrol was inexpensive, and the car was more economical than frequent bus journeys. We prayed about what to do, and the Congregational minister came round with a proposal. He'd been offered a new car for £60. Would we like to buy his old one for £30? The car in question was a Ford Popular like the deceased, but a lot younger. However, such a big hole in our bank balance would mean a very lean summer.

We bought the car.

And the inevitable happened. We ran out of food and money a month before the next expected grant cheque.

'Actually,' I said to John as we reassessed the situation during our morning prayers, 'there is still some money in the sideboard. If you remember, we didn't know where to send all the tithe from the last grant cheque, so we left it in there until the Lord showed us where it was to go.'

'Oh no!' said John quickly. 'We can't give our tithe with one hand, then snatch it back with the other. In fact, I was going to ask you about sending it to the missionary society.'

Two Bootle friends had recently begun their training as missionaries. The idea had crossed my mind too. The tithe wasn't ours, then.

'Look,' said John finally, 'we've prayed about our situation. God knows about it. Let's just trust him to do what's best.' He kissed me and the baby, and went down to the street door, ready to collect the car from the nearby car-park and drive to Oxford with what petrol was left in it.

But I didn't hear the door open.

Instead, John came back up the stairs again.

'We've had a letter,' he said.

I saw the buff envelope and sighed. 'Oh dear. Not a bill?'

'No. It's hand delivered. Just says "John and Brenda".'

It was a short note from Edmund.

'During my prayers this morning, the Lord made it clear to me that I should pay you your fee for the folksinging you did last Harvest.'

Enclosed was a cheque for five guineas.

Chapter 5

✣ Darkness to Light

When everything came crashing down around me, it was easy to blame a bereavement.

We were living in the bungalow vacated by the last of the Baptist student-pastors. Our Baptist friends had offered it to us at a very low rent and we took it gratefully because it was small, cheap to heat, and had a garden. My mother came for Christmas and was thrilled with it. After our flat in Toxteth, then another flat over a shop, I suppose she thought the bungalow was more like a 'proper' home.

As we looked ahead into the New Year things looked brighter than ever. I was expecting a spring baby, the evangelistic committee was planning a summer tent mission, and we'd already booked our usual 'Crazy Gang' holiday together in Dorset.

My mother took ill after returning to Liverpool from her visit. The whole city was in the grip of a flu epidemic, but Mum had a weak chest and was ill-equipped to fight it. After several weeks in the hospital where she'd been confined for my own birth during the war, she died there on my twenty-eighth birthday.

I was shattered. My mother had been young at heart and pretty. It seemed a very unfair death. But although I grieved as I sorted through her things, I had to keep looking forward. I was booked into the maternity hospital in a matter of weeks.

New home, new baby.

Simeon arrived in April and was soon sitting in on committees and prayer-meetings as I carried on as usual, fitting in his feeds as discreetly as possible.

By the time evangelist 'Uncle' Ken Brighton arrived with

his tent in July, it seemed unfair to blame the baby's arrival for the way I was feeling. Simeon was three months old. How could I have post-natal depression this late? It must be delayed grief, I decided, that made me so tired, so weepy, so suspicious of people's motives. I'd soon shake it off.

Knowing that grief was a 'respectable' reason for being depressed didn't help me to get rid of the depression. I had to acknowledge other irritations that worried me. I was sure some members of the fellowship thought John and I were a pain in the neck. And what about that new Christian couple from the caravan park? He was unnaturally morose, I thought, and his wife seemed to have designs on my husband. And then there was the new vicar. Since Edmund retired 'they' had sent us a man who was embarrassed by the activities of the evangelistic committee. Or so I thought. I was under a constant cloud of worry and suspicion.

Even John and I were at loggerheads. He'd come to a plateau in his thesis and was bored and disinclined to get on with it. Yet he was spending more and more time in Oxford, playing his trumpet with various ensembles and orchestras. This brought in useful extra cash, but it seemed all wrong to me so I nagged him unmercifully.

The fellowship holiday only served to put all my 'people' problems under a microscope, and even the very successful tent mission left us with added complications. 'Uncle' Ken left behind a handful of newly-converted Christians whom the four churches were pleased to welcome, and about seventy enthusiastic children with no formal Sunday school connections who were much more of a problem. The Baptists decided to run a Tuesday night club for these 'mission kids' but their small congregation just hadn't the manpower to handle them.

Meanwhile, our new vicar seemed to be finding ways of saying he wouldn't be needing any further help from John and me with the Anglican young people.

Our Baptist friends, although quite swamped by the new youngsters, and seeing us without a 'slot' at the parish church, never once took advantage of the fact that we were living in their little 'manse' by asking us to join their church and help them. I know now that it was because they understood our commitment to the Church of England and John's sense of 'call' to the Anglican ministry, but at the time I wondered if they'd rather we didn't join them.

Looking to the time when his doctorate would be finished, John went to talk and pray with our vicar about the possibility of ordination. He was assured of a speedy contact with the Diocesan Director of Ordinands.

'I'll let you know when I've been in touch,' said the vicar. And that was the last we heard of it. It was very disheartening, to say the least, and confirmed what I already thought — that nobody liked us at all. My depression deepened and I withdrew into the role of disillusioned spectator.

John was flawlessly faithful at keeping our morning and evening prayer-times going, but as I sank deeper into the depression I grew less and less interested in spiritual things. He'd read the prescribed Bible passage for the day. I would look out of the window. When he commented on the notes in the printed booklet, I 'ummed' and nodded listlessly. When he prayed for our fellowship, our friends, our family, for me, I examined the hairs on the back of his hands.

I never once thought that there was no God, or that Christianity was a sham. I knew deep down that I'd entered into a covenant relationship with God through Jesus Christ and that he would not renegue on that. It was just that it all seemed so distant and irrelevant, somehow. I felt as though I were trapped inside an old lantern whose windows were smoke-blackened and whose light had burned out. The windows couldn't be cleaned by people on the outside and I hadn't the energy to set about cleaning them from the inside.

'Leave me alone!' was my silent cry.

Increasing trouble with indigestion dulled any interest in food and I began to lose weight. But it was as well that John and the others didn't leave me alone when my symptoms became physically painful. The surgeon at the hospital diagnosed a long-standing diseased gall-bladder and prescribed hospital treatment to reduce the internal inflammation followed by an operation to remove the offending organ. Then there'd be a period of convalescence.

It couldn't have happened at a worse time. John had come to the end of his three-year studentship and had started working full-time at the local military college. What on earth should we do with the children? Our friends stepped in before we had time to ask them. Gavin went for a holiday with Bobbie and Tony where he'd often stayed before. Simeon, at five months, became the latest 'live' dolly in the girls' pram at Len and Barbara's, and took the change from breast-feeding to bottle without a whimper.

'You won't know a thing', the nurses told me as they wheeled me down to the theatre. 'You'll just fall asleep, and next minute you'll wake up back in your bed in the ward.'

I never told them how wrong they were.

For a start, it was more than just 'falling asleep'. When I succumbed to the anaesthetist's pin-prick I was transported to a world so different from the one I'd left that there wasn't even the faintest memory to remind me of it.

Yet this new world wasn't new in the sense of being unfamiliar. Quite the contrary, I was filled with a sense of being fully 'at home' in this space-world of yellow sunlight filled with floating golddust. This was so much my home, I would swear I had never once left it, never once even briefly visited any other existence. I had been here forever, would remain here forever and would not want it otherwise. My contentment was not passive however, but spiced with hope and excitement as I contemplated drawing nearer to the distant source of the sunlight that surrounded me. Somewhere just ahead (I'd be there soon) the light was magnetically intense, flashing and bouncing off the thickening golddust, and I longed to be drawn into it.

Suddenly, I was startled by noises from another place. A

note of alarm jarred my golden peace and I looked about to see the cause. Something was happening below me.

'There! How's that? Any sign?'

'No, nothing! Still nothing!'

'Oh my God! Come on. Come on!'

Above this exchange, I was no more than some kind of floating emotion. I now changed from irritation at the intrusion into my contentment to curiosity as I watched the scene below.

Slowly, it seemed, the panic rose to touch me and I realized what was going on. The surgeon and the anaesthetist wanted me to breathe.

I knew at once what that would mean. If I breathed for them, I should have to leave the sun, the gold, the peace and the hope that was more of a 'home' than I'd ever known. Worse, it would mean I should have to rejoin some awful forgotten place where I had been distressed.

No. Not that. Where's the gold? Where's the light?

A voice shouted quietly, the whispered shout of ultimate desperation.

'Oh please, *please*! For God's sake, come on!'

Confusion gave way to compassion. I'd have to breathe for them. How could I refuse?

Very deliberately, knowing fully what I was doing, and what it was costing, I took a deep breath.

I drew it somewhere near the ceiling.

I expelled it from the table.

The shouts of relief hit my ears in stereo.

'That's it! She's there!'

'Thank God! For a minute I thought . . .'

I disappeared into blackness and woke in the recovery ward.

After being moved to a quiet convalescent hospital I had plenty of time to ponder on my experience. Perhaps such 'dreams' were common. But other patients had spoken only of going to sleep and waking back in bed. I hesitated to share my own story for fear of ridicule or, from the staff, professional reassurance intended to refute all thought of theatre crises.

But I believed then, and still do, that I had indeed hovered between this life and the next, and that I had been allowed to return to my family. I know that if I'd been drawn into that light-source I'd never have been tempted away from it. I wouldn't have heard the panic, or even known I'd ever lived anywhere else but in that sublime light.

So I asked myself, as I sat outside in the autumn sun and watched the apples drop quietly from the trees in the hospital orchard: 'Why am I here and not there?'

Of course, it was impossible to formulate a specific answer beyond acknowledging that it must be part of God's will for me and my family. Whatever future God had planned for John and the children, I was to be part of it.

One thing did impress itself on me, though. I was sure God wouldn't want me to withdraw from the warmth of his eternal light just to sit inside a cold, dark lantern. The surprising thing was that the lantern seemed to have disappeared altogether. I could feel the September sun.

My convalescence was slow. I'd lost a stone before the operation and more since. Walking was painful and my innards took months to settle themselves comfortably. But I was glad to be rid of the depression.

Back home, the Baptists were still desperate for help. Shortly after Simeon's baptism, and after a lot of prayer and heart-searching, we started worshipping at the Baptist chapel and helping with the youth work.

The move was misunderstood by some and welcomed by others in both churches.

'What about your call?' I asked John, hating to phrase the words.

'Look, angel,' he said quietly, 'when we came to Faringdon we were prepared to worship and work wherever the Lord wanted us, right?'

I remembered writing down the times of services from the four churches' notice-boards.

'If the Lord's calling me to the Anglican ministry eventually, and if he wants me to spend time with the Baptists first, then he must have his reasons. Don't worry.'

I don't suppose we can guess at a tenth of those reasons even now, but during our two years as Baptists there were glimpses of possible whys and wherefores. As we relaxed in the freedom of non-liturgical worship, for example, we found ourselves missing the Anglican structures that had often chafed before.

'Wasn't it odd having no corporate confession? And why was the sermon on 'Titus in Crete' when it's Passion Sunday?'

On the other hand, because the Baptist chapel hadn't even a student-pastor at this time, depending instead on its own lay leadership, John was given opportunities for ministry he'd never have had at the parish church. As one of the four on the 'preaching and worship' team, he was either leading the worship or preaching every Sunday at one of the services. He also took his turn teaching at the midweek Bible study and prayer meeting.

At the same time, we were still working closely with our friends on the evangelistic committee, doing a house-to-house visitation of the town, and planning a gospel barbecue in the ancient tithe-barn in a nearby village.

It had been a rough year but things seemed to have settled at last. Or had they? Everything on the surface was 'back to normal', but there was still one problem I had to sort out.

Perhaps it was because of the long months when I'd been totally lacking any interest in prayer or Bible-reading, but I felt now that there was something of a gulf between me and my Heavenly Father. I'd stepped away from his counsel, and now, despite my hospital experience, I couldn't seem to get right back to that close personal relationship I'd known years before.

One evening when John was out I decided to read through the Psalms. As these are the expression of one person's relationship with God, I thought they might provide some stepping-stones to get *me* back once more to that close relationship with him.

The children were asleep, and I played some favourite records as I read quietly in the evening light. At first I read quickly and silently. Then gradually I began to read the words more slowly, speaking them out aloud. Finally, as I came to the marvellously joyful psalms of praise in the 'hundreds', the words I voiced became loud and heartfelt, as perhaps they had been for the Jews who first used them in their temple. The 'Sanctus' from Verdi's *Requiem* was a fitting accompaniment.

The adoration was as real now in my heart as it was strong on my lips and I laughed with pleasure at the thrill of uninhibited praise. I wanted to tell God again and again how much I loved him. Suddenly, the praise in my heart couldn't wait for the words of the psalms to provide expression. It erupted of its own accord like a fountain of joy from my lips, in words of its own making.

In this unexpected gift of 'tongues' I discovered all the instant spontaneity of a child who hugs a parent in sheer delight. Years before I'd asked God for this particular gift of his Spirit and nothing had happened, so I assumed then that the gift 'wasn't for me' and had forgotten all about it.

Later I would discover other facets of this new jewel. The subtle unlearned harmonies that swell from a congregation singing their praises in tongues. The clarion call to attention of a message from God given to his people in tongues, before an interpretation. The laser surgery of the Spirit, pinpointing long-buried wounds now exposed (for healing) by tongues used in personal meditation.

But now, in this solitary moment when I needed a deep assurance of my Father's closeness, the gift was his way of saying: 'Look, I'm this close. Right within you, helping you to praise me. We're all right, you and me.'

And that's all I was waiting to know.

Chapter 6

✣ Coal-tips, Kids and a Calling

We knew we couldn't hog the Baptists' bungalow forever. One day they would need it for someone else. So when John, still working on his thesis without a grant, took a school teaching job with a respectable salary, we began to pray about the possibility of buying our own home. Our friends were praying, too, that God would show us what he wanted us to do about the situation.

Our midweek Bible study and prayer meeting went 'round the houses' week by week, and one Tuesday evening when it was at our bungalow, just before we began a time of intercession, Len said: 'A friend in Swindon has asked us to pray for a retired couple he knows. They've been running a Christian bookshop, but the accommodation over the top goes with the job, so they'll have to move out very soon. They're neither of them too well, so what they need is somewhere small, with no stairs, and not too much garden. Preferably near a Baptist church.'

As we prayed, I opened one eye and peered across the room at John. He was looking at me and smiling. So the Lord wanted our bungalow! We'd better get on and find our own house.

The next day, John contacted a building society offering 100% mortgages to schoolteachers. But there was a rather tricky condition. The property had to be brand new and cost less than £4,000. Even in 1972 that was something of a tall order.

'It looks like a choice between Wigan and Lincolnshire', said John, surveying the mounds of leaflets and newspapers all over the dining table.

I didn't state a preference, partly because I knew little of either area other than the old 'Wigan Pier' jokes, but mainly because I knew our choice would be determined ultimately by the availability of jobs.

'There's a French post going at Upholland in Lancashire', came the announcement from behind the *Times Educational Supplement.*

'Is that anywhere near Wigan?' I asked.

It was, and John got the job, so we moved to a small brand-new semi on the edge of the town, torn between sadness at leaving our Faringdon friends and excitement in anticipation of discovering God's will for us in Wigan.

Our new environment was a study in contrasts. Neat new houses stood cheek by jowl with derelict terraces. Smart new shops spawned by the recent influx of residents were sandwiched between the boarded up stores that had died with the closure of the local coal pits. The surrounding countryside was enriched by the 'flash' lakes left by the mine-workings but marred by the glowering slag-heaps.

The traffic on the canal at the bottom of our garden was an assortment of coal barges, pleasure craft and swans, and the contrasts continued into the houses themselves, where the occupants were a mixture of local people glad to escape the terraces without leaving their native land, and families from Liverpool, glad to find cheap private housing within commuting distance of their home city.

The parish church was a huge red brick turn-of-the-century reminder of the area's former prosperity. The chunks of brick that occasionally fell from its pinnacles as the foundations slowly subsided were a present reminder of the area's more recent decay.

When we met the vicar and his wife on their return from their post-Easter break, they greeted us with genuine warmth tinged with a hint of incredulity. Over a 'getting to know you' cup of tea in the vicarage we learned from John and Joan that they had hoped to find a new parish during their holiday, but had been unsuccessful.

'We've only been here four years,' said our new vicar, 'but

to be honest it's been very discouraging. So we prayed to the Lord very specifically. Would he either send us someone new to help and encourage us, or move us to somewhere else.'

Joan passed a plate of biscuits. 'We've looked at two parishes in the last few weeks, but nothing's come of either of them', she said. 'So we came home wondering whether some new help was on its way!'

Well, we were new arrivals, and we were willing, and if that made us the answer to the vicar's prayers we had no objections.

So once again we were back in the Anglican church, and back in the Liverpool diocese if not in the city itself.

Almost before we'd finished unpacking, the vicar rounded us up with other church people to volunteer as helpers at a huge pop festival to be held on the edge of the parish. With Christians from other local churches we were lectured on one-to-one evangelism, how to counsel sophisticated teenagers, how to recognize the effects of drug-taking and how to comfort and control someone on a 'bad trip'. The organizers of the festival welcomed us officially, and supplied more than enough free passes, assuring us that the more Christians they could get on to the campus the better would be the 'vibes' and the less would be the hassle with the 'fuzz'.

As the thousands and thousands of 'flower power children' trekked through the streets towards the festival site in the Friday evening sunshine, the locals sat on their garden walls to watch the free carnival. Denims and kaftans, headbands and bare feet, more beads than flowers and uniform long hair, the hippie trail meandered peacefully behind their cloud of pot smoke, heading for their promised land, intent on making 'love not war' for a whole weekend.

Meanwhile, working on the premise that even transcendental meditation has to stop for meal breaks, the local fish and chip shop proprietor doubled his prices and dreamed of retiring to Blackpool.

But everyone's dreams took a dowsing when the weather broke overnight, and Saturday found us all, hippies and helpers alike, slithering about in a quagmire. From our 'Jesus tent' we dispensed hot drinks and charity clothes with our gospel leaflets. It all felt very reminiscent of the early days of the Salvation Army.

The rock music groups were seemingly unaffected by the weather on their enormous covered platform, so against the relentless 'thud-thud' of the bands and 'drip-drip' of the rain, we ripped the sleeves out of ladies' dresses from the charity clothes, knotted the ends and gave them out with poly bags as waterproof footwarmers, taking turns to go off in twos into the crowd to engage in 'evangelistic encounters'.

And surprising encounters some of them turned out to be, too.

Like the very hairy young man in the elaborately embroidered kaftan who listened intently to the claims and promises of Jesus. He sat deep in thought for several minutes then announced with startling finality: 'Okay. I'll buy that. I'm sick of this so-called search for peace and happiness anyway. It's all a big con. If Jesus gives peace and hope without drugs, I want to know Jesus.'

And he suddenly took off his luxuriant hair, which turned out to be a wig!

'I'm a bank clerk', he explained. 'I thought Christianity was just for old ladies and that the hippies had all the answers. Only you can't follow the hippies in a lounge suit!'

Then there were the 'spaced-out' young schoolteachers, smoking marijuana rolled in strips of local authority art department sugar-paper. Not all our hippies were dropouts, by a long shot.

On Saturday afternoon, American evangelist Arthur Blessit arrived to help us. Even before he opened his mouth to preach, he was an attractive spectacle, tall and tanned and immaculately dressed in white shirt and trousers, and a blue denim jacket with an enormous orange 'Jesus sticker' on the back.

He gave us a pep talk in the Jesus tent, and the love he had for those drug-happy rock fans just flowed from him as he spoke. He couldn't wait to get out into the crowds to tell them how much Jesus loved them too.

'But I guess first things first, huh?' he said in his Bible-belt American. 'Let us *all* pray!' And without a second's demur, he dropped to his knees in the mud, his other-worldly humility challenging our vanity as we reluctantly committed our already-scruffy jeans to the same miry fate.

Outside the tent, Arthur stood on a chair to preach to a largely appreciative audience. The only heckler was a young shaven-headed Hare Krishna devotee in the typical saffron robe of his cult.

'Sir,' said the evangelist patiently, after battling against the Krishna shouts for several minutes, 'if you wish to share your faith with me, I'll gladly talk with you just as soon as I've finished preaching. If you wish to preach your faith to these young people, I'll surely lend you my chair. But right now I'd ask you kindly to allow these folks to hear about my Lord and how he loves them.'

Whether or not the heckler was startled by this mild response I couldn't say, but he stopped shouting and stayed to listen.

There wasn't so much rain during Saturday night. It was cold under the starlit sky, and the ground was still awash between the duckboards, but there was almost a campfire atmosphere as the fans we'd talked to about eternal life now hummed and swayed to the strains of the star band, 'The Grateful Dead'.

In the way of all circuses, the festival 'village' decamped and disappeared during Sunday night and local life got back to normal.

Normal for us was our new semi-detached existence. John went off daily to work and Simeon at two was still at home with me, but Gavin, nearly six, ventured very shyly into the local infants' school, where he had the disadvantage of being neither local nor Liverpudlian.

Within days, he'd acquired enough 'Wiganese' to get by, but he pleaded with us about his appearance. 'Please can I have short hair and long trousers? At school if they can't see your ears and they can see your knees, they think you must be a little girl!'

Knowing how unkind children can be to 'the odd one out' we managed to give Gavin a complete change of image overnight. Though we drew the line at 'bovver boots'!

Our estate was on the southern tip of the parish and the church was near its northern boundary, a twenty minute uphill walk away. This meant that few newcomers made the effort on Sundays, so our vicar suggested we might 'do something' in our house for the estate children at least. We'd noticed there weren't a lot of children about the estate on Sundays anyway. Many families spent the day visiting relatives. Consequently, it seemed more sensible for us to 'do something' midweek.

John and I went from house to house, just in our own road, inviting the parents to let their children come to us for an hour after tea on Wednesdays. At not one home did we meet any opposition or even hesitation.

Every week we had about twenty children of between two and fourteen years at our 'Wednesday Club'. We ran it like a Sunday school, with songs and games, prayers and puzzles, Bible stories and activities all based on the 'all-ages' syllabus we'd sent for by post.

The children loved to sing to John's guitar, and when we heard of a song contest on BBC Radio Merseyside to promote Christian Aid, it seemed a good idea to have a go. I wrote a bouncy chorus song on the set theme 'Joy for the World' and we taught it to the children, explaining that we hoped to enter them for the competition. Finally, when it was as good as we could get it, John dangled a microphone from the electric lamp shade and we sang our new song on to the tape recorder.

'Now we'll have to listen to Sunday's broadcast to see if we're in the finals,' he said, and he popped the tape into a padded envelope ready for posting.

Doorbells up and down the road worked overtime on the Sunday.

'Did you hear us? Did you hear our Wednesday Club song on the radio? That was us, you know! We're in the last six!'

The winner was to be decided by postcard votes from the programme's listeners. Suddenly all those aunts, uncles and grannies the children visited at weekends became very important!

'Don't forget to send your postcard in, Gran! We want to win!'

Well, we didn't quite win. We came second. It meant our song was broadcast yet again, by which time the children's excitement was tempered by professional self-criticism.

'There's you, Claire, on the wrong note!'

'Shh! Listen to the next bit. That's where Lee fell off the piano stool!'

As runners-up, we were to be presented with our prize by the Lord Mayor of Liverpool. Most of the children were able to get to the ceremony, which was just as well, because a handshake from the golden-chained gentleman was much more awe-inspiring than one-twentieth of a £2 book token!

Our friends at the Tuesday night Bible study group at the vicarage followed our 'Wednesday Club' activities with interest, supporting us fully with their prayers (and their postcards!). With some of the other men, John took his turn in preparing the weekly Bible study, and as he taught us from the Scriptures I began to realize what a debt we owed to our time in Faringdon. We'd learned so much during our years there in fellowship with Christians from different backgrounds, and John's talks were always coloured by the breadth of vision gained from our Faringdon experience.

Inevitably (I suppose), our vicar eventually posed the question, 'What would you say to the idea of full-time ministry?'

As we were 'proper' Anglicans again, the matter had to come off the shelf we'd consigned it to during our Baptist years. John's thesis was at last completed, and our vicar was eager to arrange an interview with the Diocesan Director of Ordinands.

All the old obstacles had gone. But now a new one presented itself. John's job was no longer just a means to an end whilst he researched his thesis. He'd been awarded his doctorate. Now his school pupils were sailing through their own exams with some distinction. He was loving every minute in teaching, the kids obviously liked him too, and he was beginning to be 'mentioned in despatches' at Governors' meetings. In short, teaching suited him, and promised to be a more than satisfactory career.

But as we prayed the call persisted.

We were meeting up with old north country friends after our time in the south. Dave, the ordinand we'd known in Bootle, now had his own church here in Wigan after a curacy in Toxteth. The curate who'd married us in Bootle was now a vicar in Liverpool after a second curacy in Wigan!

And both of them asked: 'What are you doing about ordination?'

So, encouraged on all sides, John went through the various interviews and finally to the compulsory residential selection conference.

Candidates are informed by their bishop whether or not they have been recommended for ministerial training by the interviewing board. John's letter from the Bishop of Liverpool, Stuart Blanch, seemed to have been written with as much bewilderment as we felt on reading it. Not only had John not been recommended, but the selectors had taken the rare option of not even suggesting he might approach them again after some interval spent gaining appropriate experience or correction.

An out-of-hand rejection was virtually unheard of! It

shook us, to say the least, and made us ashamed of our arrogance in assuming the selection board would automatically recognize the validity of John's call. If the lesson in humility were the only benefit of the jolt, we needed it. We were disappointed, of course. I think we were even prepared to accept that John had been wrong, that the Lord wasn't calling him to full-time ministry.

But we both hoped there'd been a mistake.

The bishop sent for him, to try to discover what had gone wrong.

'They say in their report that you're too dogmatic. What gave them that impression, do you think?'

'Hmm. Well, I saw someone's eyebrows go up when I told them about my conversion at Oxford. Perhaps they thought I'd expect a "datable" overnight conversion from all my parishioners?'

'Yes, possibly. Next they say they thought you were unsure of your call. What do you make of that?'

'Oh, I think I know how that may have happened. One of the questions was what would I do if I were rejected. I said I had a wife, two kids and a mortgage, so continuing in teaching would seem preferable to jumping in the river!'

'I take your point,' said the bishop, 'though they may well have thought you were being unduly frivolous. Now, why should they think your application for ordination could be a passing whim?'

John thought hard for a moment.

'I suppose you could get that impression from my application form. I mean, look at the various jobs I've had. Store management and a bit of teaching before I started the research. Then after the grant ran out I had two jobs before I went back to teaching. The lab work at the military college didn't cover our basic expenses so I sold life insurance for a while. I wasn't looking for a career. I was supporting my family while I wrote a thesis. But it does look like I've just flitted from job to job.'

'So it's not a passing whim to you, then?'

'No, sir. I've been praying about entering the full-time ministry for seven or eight years.'

After a lengthy interview, Bishop Stuart decided John had probably been misread. He advised him to apply for a new selection conference, which would consist of an entirely different interview board, and assured him that if his call were truly from the Lord, he would certainly be selected next time.

'In the meantime,' he said, 'I suggest you broaden your horizons by reading Owen Chadwick's *The Victorian Church*. Both volumes.'

When John dropped the two weighty tomes, and the hefty bill, on our table the following week, he had his work cut out convincing me he wasn't embarking on a penance!

The following year he was unconditionally recommended, and the bishop's letter of congratulation was followed by a jubilant note from the Director of Ordinands: 'The bishop and I were prepared to do a protest demo with banners, but it seems this won't be necessary!'

At school, where John's intentions had long been known, there were more congratulations, but none from the rueful headmaster. This most gracious man was an avowed non-Christian who felt John was throwing away a brilliant career. Nonetheless, he had insisted that John take promotion in his final year: 'Not to tempt you to stay, but to thank you for what you've given.'

The year's delay was not without consequence. Simeon, at four and a half, would now be able to go to school with Gavin and being 'new boys' together would make it easier for both of them.

But where?

Some crossed wires between John and the college at Bristol resulted in us thinking they'd reserved him a place (and a married student's flat) when in fact they hadn't.

While we were still in our state of blissful ignorance about this, we received a letter from the Principal of the college at Durham. He wondered why John had sent for a prospectus but hadn't followed it up with a visit, and urged us both to go and look at Durham, even if our minds were set elsewhere.

Thinking of it as an interesting pleasure trip, we arranged to drive up after school one Friday after dropping the children at John's parents', to return on the Sunday with our sights on Bristol.

On the Friday in question, John phoned me at lunchtime to query some last minute details.

'Oh, by the way,' I said, 'there's a letter for you here from Bristol.'

'Oh? I wonder what that's about? Would you open it and see?'

I did, and could hardly find words to tell him.

'Darling, there's been some kind of mistake. They say they're sorry if you had the impression they'd kept last year's arrangements on their files. All this year's places have already been filled.'

'No. That can't be right. Are you sure?'

'"We regret we have no vacancies for the coming academic year." John, what do we do now?'

'We thank the Lord for the invitation from Durham, and go and look at it in a very different light. That's what we do now!'

All the way up the A1(M) I was biting back the tears. Who wanted to live in Durham with its Miners' Gala and its pit-heaps? Why couldn't we go to Bristol? I'd promised the children we'd live near the zoo! Anyway, hadn't we seen enough pit-heaps in Wigan?

Two very small miracles smoothed our arrival in Durham and we didn't even notice them. The first was the detailed set of directions from a teaching colleague which took us to the centre of the city, round the policeman in his box (now made redundant by pedestrianization) and back on ourselves up the tiny street to the cathedral and the old colleges.

Only when we saw other drivers scratching their heads and jamming the traffic as they wondered how on earth to do this manoeuvre did we realize we'd been blessed on our first attempt! And we slid into a parking space right outside the college entrance, with just two minutes to go to our appointment with the principal. I don't think I saw that space empty once in term-time during the next three years!

The little miracles continued. Durham wasn't all coal-pits at all. It was just like Oxford, only hilly. And there were friends here, too. The curate who'd prepared me for confirmation was now a college tutor, and his wife and I were soon tripping down memory lane.

And in this city, so remote from the affluent south, even students could afford to buy houses.

Before we left for home on the Sunday, John found me reading the bits of paper on the college notice-board.

'What's caught your attention here, then?'

'Him.'

I pointed to a notice about a meeting at the Methodist church, where the minister was apparently the Methodist chaplain to the University.

'So?'

'Guess where he did his first placement after he came out of theological college?'

'No idea. You tell me.'

'Liverpool. Miss Baker's church. Thundered at us during Advent about the second coming, and sang like an angel in the tenors of the Free Churches' Choir.'

'What do you reckon to Durham, then?'

'I'd say it feels like home!'

He gave me a hug and we stepped out on to the ancient cobbles that would soon be a familiar path.

Chapter 7

❊ Singing Together in Durham

If I had once been disappointed at not living in the centre of Oxford, Durham was to redress the balance.

In this other medieval city, puckered into alleys and folds on the slopes around the great loop of the River Wear, where the castle and cathedral crown the peninsula hill, we now lived in the centre of town. At the back of our street was the bus-station, at the front the massive railway viaduct with its famous view of cathedral and city (and our terrace!). The local shops were in fact the main stores, and yet the short walk to college, through the ancient 'Abbot's vineyard' and along the wooded river bank, was a country walk I came to treasure.

Our house was in St Margaret's parish, and we soon arranged for the boys to start at the church school, so it seemed not unreasonable for us to worship at St Margaret's church itself, a flint grey twelfth-century chapel-of-ease just across the river from the cathedral.

'You won't like it!' said someone at college. 'It's not what you're used to. The one by the market would suit you better!'

'But we're parishioners!' was our response. 'It's silly to walk past your own parish church to go to another without at least giving it a try!'

Admittedly, St Margaret's was higher in its practice than we'd been used to. In the same week that we moved into our house, we went along to have a look at the church, and were welcomed by a delightful old lady who asked if we could oblige her with a match to light the sanctuary lamp. Then she put the finishing touches to the flowers and left us to explore.

The place was obviously well-loved. Everything glowed, as if taking its cue from that lamp, from the smooth stone floor and the solid oak pews to the bright whitewashed walls and the jewel-paned windows. Alongside the familiar *Ancient and Modern Revised* on the pew ledges were leaflets of newer songs that we knew. And hanging against the pillar away above the brass eagle lectern was a beautiful felt collage with the text: 'The Spirit of God was not lost after Pentecost; no, the Spirit is among us.'

The rector made us very welcome on the Sunday, and reassured us with his slogan: 'At St Margaret's we're Evangelical in our preaching, Pentecostal in our fellowship and Catholic in our worship!'

It was the last of these I found a bit difficult. At the Family Communion service each week I felt I was missing a good deal of blessing simply because I didn't understand much of the symbolism, although the friendship and joyful singing in the packed church were in themselves magnetic. It seemed stupid to persist in ignorance, especially as the children were as clueless as I was, even if John could find his way about. At last I bought a child's communion book that explained every aspect of the Anglo-Catholic tradition complete with pictures and labels. For the next few weeks I went through the service with the official Series Three communion book in one hand and my 'young person's guide' in the other!

Unfortunately, across the river from Monday to Friday, adjustments in college came a little harder, again for me if not for John. He was absolutely in his element as he embarked on his intensive course, the theology BA and a further diploma, a total of five years' study to be crammed into the three years we should be in Durham. He went from lecture to seminar to tutorial with relish, and in the upstairs study we shared at Cranmer Hall he ploughed into essay after essay with the kind of enthusiasm that engenders the necessary energy required for the task and a lot more besides.

However, within a week of the first term I was convinced I was not cut out to be the 'mature student' I'd planned on being, now that both the children were at school. For a start, all the lecturers seemed to throw out the most unnerving challenges as the opening to their particular course.

'How far is your faith built on documented knowledge of the historical person of Jesus?'

'Why, within the one Church of England, are there such variant beliefs and practices?'

'Statement: "The church in different ages has favoured different theories of atonement."'

Really?

I wondered which theory was currently in favour and whether or not I had a 'correct' appreciation of the crucifixion and resurrection of Jesus. Maybe I wasn't a proper Christian at all and wouldn't be going to Heaven? Perhaps only one church party had it properly worked out. But which one? And what about the God I related to daily? Was he my Father-Creator, the Holy Spirit, or the glorified Jesus? Did the man Jesus ever exist? Had I been conned?

With what seemed like enormous holes shot through the personal Christian experience that had sustained me for thirteen years, I sat down to write my first essay, for the church history tutor. I had marshalled all the necessary facts by way of lecture notes, suitable book extracts and my own scribbled jottings, but somehow the shock to my system of all this sudden questing and querying had petrified my brain. I could not arrange the facts into reasoned prose!

Finally, I went to the tutor concerned and confessed my dilemma.

'It's all there in bits and pieces,' I told him, 'but I think I've been away from studying too long. A shopping list seems to be the total extent of my literary skill these days.'

'Nonsense!' was his counsel.

He looked at my notes, asked me particular questions about the sequence of some events at issue, and my opinion of the people involved. Soon we were embroiled in a racy conversation of 'Don't you thinks?' and 'Oh surely nots' and 'Yes, but what abouts?'

In the end my tutor sat back and relaxed.

'There!' he said. 'I don't think you have any problems at all. Just go and write down everything you've said to me. Preface it with the phrase, "I think that . . ." if you like, then cross it out when you've written what you do think.'

It worked, in more ways than one. I got a good mark for his essay, and I never sat pen poised, stuck for words, in quite the same way again. But getting that first essay under my belt also restored some of the holes in my confidence and my faith. If there were questions to be asked, theories to be examined, then I'd ask them and examine them and give as honest and articulate an opinion as I could. And at the end of the day, I felt, I couldn't finish off any worse than I'd begun. I might even learn something!

I was the only wife attending lectures in college that year, but not the only woman by any means. Cranmer Hall was the first of the Anglican theological colleges to admit women students, and found itself far in advance of the Church of England as a whole, who didn't know quite how to examine and assess these women training to be parish workers or deaconesses.

The 'lowest common denominator' in academic training for men was, and is, the General Ordination Examination in a number of prescribed subjects. Candidates can fly a bit higher by reading for university diplomas or degrees, but they're still examined in any GOE subjects not covered by their other studies. So while it was 'GOE Rules OK?' for the men, the women could not be dealt with in quite the same way lest it should be thought they were being prepared for ordination! In the early days of women's training, ordination was not even a remote possibility.

Cranmer Hall solved the problem by entering its women candidates for the external Cambridge Certificate in Religious Knowledge, known then as CRK. This covered sufficient parallel ground as to allow students to be taught together. CRK suited me, too, as it was a recognized further qualification for trained teachers. So I joined the GOE men with the other CRK women.'

Perhaps it was because this group had all the high flyers like John creamed off to do their degrees and what-have-you, that we gelled into an unthreatened and harmonious fellowship of men and women of all ages, where good humour was the order of the day.

An Irish tutor who lectured us in Old Testament began every session by dashing off a sketch map of the Holy Land on the blackboard. He would then trace, with a hasty dotted line, the descent into Egypt, the Exodus, and the route back to the Promised Land, before picking up the story where he'd left it the week before.

One session, he arrived to find that someone had already drawn his map for him.

'Ah! Now that speeds things up a bit,' he beamed. 'Thank you!'

And he proceeded to do his dotted-line round tour as usual. There were many smiles and stifled giggles when his chalk crossed one Red Sea, only to find itself on the shores of a second one!

The lecturer paused, chalk held firm to the board. Then he shrugged.

'Sure, what's another miracle?' he muttered, and dotted on to complete his journey.

Then there was the dour Scot who lectured New Testament and informed us of a fifth Gospel.

'The apocryphal Gospel of Thomas,' he intoned in his melodious Highland accent, 'written in Coptic.'

Behind me, the male nurse from Lancashire asked the former children's nanny from Liverpool: 'Eh, Lynne, what's Coptic?'

'It's a language,' she said. 'It goes "Ee-aye-addio-we-won-the-cup" and they speak it on the Kop at Anfield Football Ground. You know, Koptic!'

On the whole I was well accepted by the other students, although some of the singles were a little resentful of married students as a genus because we couldn't enter fully into the residential life of the college.

Fair comment.

But John for one was as committed to college as he could possibly have been. His day started in chapel before breakfast and finished after college dinner in the evening, with a break at home at teatime when the children came in from school.

I stayed at college for lunch each day, but afternoons were a battle against the library clock, as I consulted the great tomes and made my notes, trying to leave enough time to do the shopping on my way to meet the children.

A tutor's wife ran a weekly Wives' Group at her home in the college complex, where the informal discussions covered all kinds of topics from cooking on a limited income to coping with tramps! Serious issues were covered too. A gynaecologist talked about abortion, and a psychiatrist talked about depression.

As wives go, we were an average selection, I suppose. Young, older, thin, fat. But because of who our husbands were, there were other traits to be noticed. Some of the shyer ones were genuinely terrified of running the Mothers' Union, or of being run by it! At the other end of the scale, some of the bolder ones were all set to run not only the Mothers' Union, the Sunday school and the playgroup, but the whole of the parish and their husbands as well! It was probably a good thing that the years of our husbands' training gave us wives time to sort ourselves out in our own group.

Not all the married ordinands' wives came to the Wives' Group, though. There were some, just a few, who considered their husband's career as his own business, and wanted no part of it either during his training or even later on in the parish. Those I managed to meet and listen to could make out a very attractive case for their independence. But I thought then, and still think, that maintaining such a position in practice in your average Church of England parish would be difficult and painful.

My friend at the Wives' Group was Val. She and Bob lived in St Margaret's parish so we were near neighbours and fellow parishioners too. Bob had in earlier years been a semi-pro rock guitarist and before long the four of us were spending our evenings playing and singing together, the two men on their guitars and Val and I singing along.

When some of our St Margaret's friends were arranging a day of renewal in Newcastle, they asked John if he could supply the music to accompany the choruses. So the four of us made our first public appearance as a music group.

It was hard work, in that we were leading a thousand people in the singing, but we made some important discoveries that day. On the plus side, we found we were confident leaders, able to give a really solid support for the singing. We found, too, that we were thinking as one when it came to spontaneous key-changes or repeats. But most important, we discovered how to listen to the Holy Spirit as Director of Music. That may seem a bit flippant, but in fact it became the most crucial element of our music together in the months that followed, this constantly praying while playing and singing.

For example, maybe we had learned a song in the key of G. Why should we then feel compelled on occasions to introduce it in F? Or A? We could never be sure. Sometimes a change of key would allow a direct link into another song important to the meeting. Sometimes we saw in retrospect that the ethos of the meeting had been subtly altered, say from praise to penitence, and the key-changes had helped to facilitate this transition. Gradually the four of us learned to listen as one, to be obedient to the Spirit's leading, and to just wait and see. Above all, we learned to be sensitive rather than manipulative.

Our first public outing had one big minus, however. We were definitely under-powered, with only two acoustic guitars and four voices. And yet before we left that first meeting in Newcastle, we'd been inundated with requests to play at other meetings, some of them just as large.

That evening, we prayed together about the whole business.

'Lord, if you're calling us to minister regularly in this way, you know that we need more equipment. And you know that we're on very tight budgets. Please guide us and supply our needs.'

Later, when people commented on our superb equipment — two new acoustic guitars, electric bass, electric piano, seven microphones on five stands, amplifiers, speakers and echo unit, all neatly packed into a specially fitted minibus — Bob was prone to say: 'It just fell through the letterbox after we prayed!'

What he meant was that suddenly, it seemed to us, the small ads in the local free paper were crammed with group equipment, exactly the bits and pieces we were looking for. Bob's experience in the pop world was invaluable here, as he selected one particular item whilst disregarding three or four similar offers. It was amazing. The paper would arrive. We'd spot something we needed for our music ministry, and we'd pray about it. Then within days one or other of us would receive a cheque to cover the cost. These sums of money were unsolicited personal gifts, or tax refunds, or small charity grants we'd applied for and forgotten about long before we started singing together.

Within a month of that first meeting we were 'on the road' as 'Electric Fish — Band Together For Jesus'.

All four of us sang. John played guitar or trumpet. Bob played guitar or spoons! Val was a 'natural' on tambourine and I played bass guitar or piano or (occasionally) tuba. Our repertoire was dictated by the venues we played. At youth meetings we did Christian rock numbers. At Harvest socials and the like we played Christian folk and country music, with occasional 'novelty' items with the trumpet, spoons and tuba.

But our first love was leading people in worship. Nothing

thrilled us more than when a congregation so relaxed in the security of our accompaniment that they forgot we were there, and just worshipped the Lord in song, 'lost in wonder, love and praise'.

There were two notable occasions when we were asked to exercise this special ministry in Durham Cathedral.

The first was when St Margaret's church was using the cathedral for an Ascension Day celebration. We played and sang while the Sacred Dance Group from Colorado, USA praised most powerfully in movement and dance. Then we sang two songs on our own, what we called 'performance songs', where the words carried some spiritual message.

One of these songs, selected from a well-known music book, had beautiful words and a superb main tune, but we'd all felt that the middle section was a bit weak, musically. So it was with a good deal of trepidation that we had rewritten the middle for this occasion, extremely wary of tampering with someone else's work.

Just before he was due to preach, the guest speaker, Tom Smail, asked everybody to get up and greet a stranger! The four of us went off in different directions to shake hands with people we didn't know. Back in our seats, with Tom Smail preaching, I could see that Bob was excited about something other than the sermon, but there was no chance to ask him about it as it was time to lead the people in their worship and praise.

To be there in that great Norman church that had rung to centuries of hymns and psalms, to be there myself, playing and singing, and totally surrounded by the love and joy of a thousand voices adoring their Lord, was a wonderfully moving and humbling experience. I really thought the angels were with us. And maybe they were.

When the service finally finished, John asked Bob to share his secret.

'You know how bothered we were about altering that song? Well . . .'

Immediately after we'd performed the rewritten song,

and we'd all gone off to greet people, Bob had approached a gentleman in the south transept.

'Hi! I'm Bob!'

'Pleased to meet you, Bob,' said the stranger, with a broad smile. 'I'm the writer of that last song, and I must say I do prefer your 'middle eight' to mine!'

Some time later, the Christian Union promoted a student mission in Durham, with David Watson and Garth Hewitt as missioners. 'Electric Fish' was booked to lead the worship at the weekday David Watson meetings and at the final service at the cathedral, and also to open the week in a concert with Garth at one of the colleges.

We were very excited about this particular commission. Garth Hewitt, as a Durham graduate himself, was already something of an inspiration and between us we had all his records. What a privilege now to be asked to play at one of his concerts!

We had a meal together the night before the event and Garth outlined his strategy. The concert was to be something of a 'softener', aimed at students who wouldn't normally go to a religious meeting, but who might be persuaded to go to the mission meetings after an easy and enjoyable evening of Christian music in concert. The programme would open with a student group doing some of their own compositions.

'Then you go on', he said, 'and entertain them. Give them a good time. Get them laughing. We're not there to preach. Then, when I go on, I'll try and clinch it so that they'll accept an invitation to the other meetings with David. OK?'

The hall was packed to overflowing with noisy, cheerful, denim-clad rock fans long before the published time for the concert. This in itself was an answer to prayer. They settled comfortably as the first group played their easy-on-the-ear slightly Latin numbers.

Then it was us.

I don't know how I survived the shock of our first chord. It was so loud! The blast bounced off the panelled rear wall and roared back at us. John had done the sound balancing earlier, as he always did, and I thought he'd made a terrible mistake with the levels. But he hadn't. He'd guessed that the rock concert regulars would be wooed by the familiarity of decibels as much as anything else, and he was right. They loved it. We threw everything at them including the spoons (well, not literally!) and they screamed and yelled for more.

When Garth Hewitt finally topped the bill, his audience was all ears, fully appreciative of his tremendous talent and enthusiasm. Indeed, although we'd agreed we shouldn't preach, the students were so responsive to Garth's songs that we weren't a bit surprised when at the end he spoke quietly of his Saviour. It was an unexpected opportunity and very sensibly he took it and used it.

Many young people were counselled that night, and there was no difficulty in getting the others to the more serious meetings with David Watson. It's well known that 'God works in a mysterious way his wonders to perform', but there can't be many handbooks recommending funny songs with tuba and spoons as effective pre-evangelism!

As it happened, we weren't the only ones the Lord surprised that night.

Next morning we found ourselves in very serious trouble with some of our student friends. The Christian Union committee, having booked us largely to lead worship, had been appalled to see us larking about and deafening the populace with our volume control. Or lack of it! This, of course, was a million miles from the sensitive music they were hoping for on the other evenings, so they had an emergency meeting, and promptly cancelled all our other mission bookings.

However, although they preferred to manage without us, they weren't sure they could manage without our microphones, and I must say it took a fair bit of grace of the gritted teeth variety for us to let them use them!

Small meetings are one thing, but as the end of the week approached with the big mission service in the cathedral, panic must have set in. Or perhaps someone finally remembered the other service we'd done there. Anyway, a very apologetic young man came and asked us on the Saturday if we'd kindly play at the cathedral on the Sunday, but please would we not do anything funny.

He needn't have worried. Worship was our thing. So we worshipped, and so did the hundreds and hundreds of students gathered there at the end of their mission week. And after David Watson preached, many of them filed forward in an act of commitment to Jesus.

We were fortunate in having some very good friends in Durham who supported the 'Electric Fish' ministry by baby-sitting for us while we travelled about. But if we were booked for a weekend event, we usually managed to take our boys with us. Bob and Val hadn't any children just then. They did have an elderly labrador bitch though, called Chloe, so we took her too.

John and Bob did a marvellous job on the old minibus we picked up for thirty pounds. All the equipment was loaded to fit between the rear doors and an interior bulkhead that they built. There was a side door for the passengers, opening on to a carpeted central section, with leather seats and a heater. Chloe sat in front with the men, who took turns driving.

When we bought the bass guitar, in the job-lot with it came a paint-spraying gadget, so we sprayed the 'Fish Bus' bright lime green. On the side doors we painted in black our 'Electric Fish' motif, and on the rear doors we did an enormous design in red and blue. This was quite a cunning device based on an American Jesus sticker we'd seen. The words 'JESUS' and 'LOVE' were built around each other in the two colours and you were never sure which one you had read first.

The children loved going on 'Fish' outings. We took them one Saturday to a place in Yorkshire advertising an amplifier and two column speakers. When we got there, they were highly amused to find that the address was a public house, closed for the afternoon, of course. Nonetheless, the stuff was right, and cheap, so we bought it. Came 'Open Day' at the infants' school and now John and I were highly amused. For Simeon's 'diary' included a marvellous account of a trip to the pub for some gear for Dad's group, complete with picture!

Driving away from that pub, we almost left Chloe in the car-park. It was the publican's wild waving that alerted us. She was terribly huffy about it and sulked for days. So after that we put her on our loading list, the stacking order for the equipment as it went in and out of the bus. After the big items, it now read: 'Echo unit, mike box, tambourine, dog.'

Sometimes, the incongruity of a mother of two in her thirties standing behind a microphone playing a bass guitar would strike me in the middle of a song. I'd find myself performing on automatic pilot and thinking: 'What am I doing here? Why am I not a proper housewife?'

It was all right for Val. She was much younger and very pretty and a credit to any music group.

But any misgivings were quickly dispelled whenever I saw our music used by God to touch somebody.

'He must know what he's doing,' I'd think, and I'd bash on.

John and Bob had more serious doubts. Their tutors at college quite rightly wondered whether our musical activities would adversely affect their studies. It was agreed that an assessment should be made at the end of our first year, and if they appeared to be struggling, 'Electric Fish' would be disbanded.

I suppose I ought not to have been surprised at the outcome. That the Lord had called us to this music ministry had been confirmed by the way he'd equipped us. At assessment time, John and Bob were each out in front of their respective classes. Obviously, when the Lord provides, it's not just a matter of guitars and amplifiers.

Chapter 8

❋ Living Together in Durham

'It's weird, but it works!'

That was the judgement given by a local councillor about one particular aspect of church life at St Margaret's, the emphasis on community living.

He was manning the Citizens' Advice stall in Durham Market when John and Bob went to ask about welfare services in Sunderland. They'd been in that town on a short pastoral assignment and had met a handicapped teenage girl in urgent need of accommodation. The councillor, with obvious concern, wrote down all the details and promised to get his Sunderland colleagues to take up the girl's case.

'Of course, if she lived here in Durham it'd be different,' he said.

'Oh yes? Why?'

'Oh, it's not the welfare that's different. Only here in Durham there's this church, you see. They're really into caring, and I don't mean your usual hostels and soup-runs. No, they've got these houses in the parish where the families have taken extra people in to live with them. Now, if this kid lived in Durham, I could knock on any of those doors and she'd be guaranteed a proper home for as long as she wanted.'

John and Bob smiled as they recognized their parish church, but said nothing.

'They're religious, of course. Always having prayer meetings. But they'd share the shirt on their back, if asked. I can tell you, I've seen some real problem cases changed beyond recognition in those families. It's weird, but it works!'

In fact, not all the extended households in St Margaret's

parish were 'open house' care-centres, though some of them certainly were. It was recognized that accommodating 'problem cases', as the councillor called them, was a long-term commitment that could only be undertaken by families whose own stability and resourcefulness would not be threatened by the whole-hearted inclusion of a difficult brother or sister with severe problems of one sort or another.

Other St Margaret's people lived 'in community' for other reasons. Some families opened their homes to students, as family, not as tenants, with great benefit on both sides. Students who were Christians themselves appreciated the loving atmosphere of a Christian home, with the opportunity to grow in their faith amongst other believers of all ages, not just their peers. For non-Christian students, it was a chance to see how Christian couples operate in good times and bad, what makes a Christian marriage and family 'tick'. The nuclear family gained from the enthusiasm and fun the students brought, and not least from the easing of the baby-sitting burden. How many young couples without the support of an extended household would have the opportunity to go together to church and to meetings on a regular basis?

This kind of community living was the church's way of replacing the old 'natural' extended family of grandmas and in-laws which has been largely fragmented these days, as we've become a more mobile and more insular people generally. Some 'additions' were ex-students or had never been students. Of these, some worked at regular jobs and gave financial support to their household. Others worked full-time in the church and community, supported by their household. The smallest extended family consisted of two single women! But when Phyllis, an older lady who lived alone in a large apartment since the death of her parents, invited into her home young Susan, a very bouncy newly qualified French teacher, they both saw it as an opportunity. An opportunity to develop, or curb, areas of their personality that would otherwise have been neglected.

John and I and our two boys were spending so much time with Bob and Val (and Chloe!) that we began to feel like one family. Indeed, the time came when Stephen, our rector, took to referring to us as 'a household'. We ate together, shopped together, went out together, stayed in together, laughed together and prayed together. And just like any people who love each other, we resented being parted at the end of the day!

'It's stupid', we'd say, 'maintaining two houses just for the sake of a bedroom annexe up the hill!'

Since ours was a two-bedroomed house and theirs was an even tinier cottage with only one proper bedroom, the idea of us all squashing into one of these homes was too ludicrous to consider. Instead, we went looking for a new house, large enough for us all and a few extras as well.

One day over college lunch, Bob said: 'How d'you fancy living in a big Georgian terrace house, three storeys plus garage, six bedrooms, three reception, cathedral views, etcetera, etcetera?'

Val narrowed her eyes suspiciously, fork halted twixt plate and mouth.

'Did the Lord give you that picture?'

John answered before Bob could.

'I doubt it! It sounds just like the empty house a few doors down from the rectory!'

'Nice though,' Bob pressed, 'and it's not actually up for sale. I reckon it must be dean and chapter, like Phyllis's place.'

Suddenly I was interested.

'You mean they'd let it? We might rent it?'

We all looked to John as head of household, so it was he who was sent off to discuss the matter with Stephen, and between them they composed a careful letter to the dean and chapter of the cathedral. We waited impatiently for the outcome, but in the meantime we had other accommodation problems.

Bob had undertaken to find properties in Durham for

new married ordinands coming to Cranmer Hall. Couples with children liked to get settled into their new homes in time for the beginning of the school term, so it came as a great blow to one family when the house they were hoping to buy was suddenly withdrawn from the market.

Bob felt badly about their problem, although he wasn't at all to blame for the sale falling through.

'How can we possibly get them installed in Durham, even temporarily, in time for school?' he pleaded, to us and to the Lord.

We prayed together, knowing full well that the family concerned were praying just as hard at their end.

'If we got that house by the rectory, they could come and live there with us,' Val said.

'Or they could have our house,' I offered. 'I mean, they mightn't fancy community living.'

'Especially with the likes of us!' John was obviously thinking of our tendency to burst into four-part harmony halfway through a meal.

But the letter from the dean and chapter, when it came, regretted that the house in question was not available to the general public.

'Now what?' Bob wailed.

'How about if they came to live with us in our house while they look for their own place?' I ventured, more out of Christian duty than real willingness.

'That's not really practical, angel,' John said gently. 'We don't know each other. Just imagine, four adults, four boys, two bedrooms.'

'Well, we can't ask them to stay with us either,' Val frowned, 'with only one bedroom. Especially strangers.'

Bob began to chuckle. 'We wouldn't be strangers long, though! Four adults, two kids and a dog, all on top of each other!'

While we were all laughing, an idea half-formed itself in my mind, then vapourized voluntarily, finding itself in the category of Things Already Considered And Dismissed.

Something made me summon it back again for further examination.

'Hey! You'd never get four adults, two kids and a dog in *your* place,' I said, 'but you could just in *our* place, with a squeeze.'

John shook his head.

'We've been through that. They don't even know us.'

'I didn't mean *them*,' I countered. 'I meant *us*. The four of us, living in our house. We know each other. Then this new couple could squash into Bob and Val's cottage until they find another house to buy. We'd all be a bit cramped, in both houses, but it would only be temporary.'

So we did get to live together, Bob and Val and ourselves, only it wasn't in the larger house we'd assumed would be necessary. They found an extra set of bunk beds to add to the ones our boys slept in, in our front bedroom, and rang the new ordinand to say his family could come to Durham just as soon as they wanted.

He was delighted, of course, but there were other reactions.

'You're *what*?' Stephen's eyebrows took off when John told him of our new sleeping arrangements.

'We're leaving our boys undisturbed in their own bunks. Brenda and I are alternating with Bob and Val in the other bunks. A week in the bunks, a week in the double bed in the back bedroom.'

'Well, I haven't seen that one in any of the charismatic paperbacks!' he quipped. But his brow was furrowed.

All our college friends thought the set-up was hilarious.

'You take turns?' blinked one incredulous inquirer. 'What do you do? Ring a bell halfway through the night?'

And if either of the men seemed the slightest bit out of sorts, someone would ask: 'What's the matter? Your week in the bunks, is it?'

After four or five weeks, Stephen arranged for another household to lend us their bed-settee in exchange for our fixed sofa. So now we took turns between the upstairs proper double bed and the downstairs bed-settee. A distinct improvement!

No one thought to ask Chloe what she thought about community living. With her own dog-basket and a lot of extra fuss from Gavin and Simeon, she seemed happy enough. In fact, I found she smiled quite a bit. Perhaps all golden Labradors do.

When 'Electric Fish' was asked to play at a bonfire and barbecue on November 5, we took the boys, but left Chloe indoors. We also travelled in two vehicles, the men in the bus with the equipment, and Val and me in the car with the children, so that we could come home ahead of the men and get the boys to bed.

After a happy evening of singing and sausages, Val and I arrived home with two very sleepy kids, only to discover we hadn't a doorkey between us.

'Nothing for it but to break in,' I said. 'You stay out here with the boys till I open up.'

'Watch out for Chloe!' Val warned, as I climbed out of the car. 'I'm not sure how she'll be with burglars, especially if she's been frightened by fireworks!'

I scaled the back wall without too much difficulty and found a long piece of wire in the shed. The dustbin made a step up to the flat roof of the kitchen, and then came the hard bit. I'd have to wriggle far enough through the small transom window of the bathroom to be able to reach down and unhook the latch of the main window, fighting off a mad dog while I did it!

Chloe didn't come to investigate the noise until I was half in, half out of the little window, balanced on my tummy. Then, the bathroom door pushed open and she padded in. She looked up, saw it was me, and smiled!

'You're supposed to see me off!' I scolded, while saying a silent prayer of thanks that she hadn't.

By Christmas, our new college friends had bought a house of their own and Bob and Val moved back to their cottage. We were all glad of the extra space, and pleased to note that our 'sardine' period had produced none of the friction some of our friends had forecast. And some of the people at church probably never even knew that we'd had any change in our circumstances at all, because we still did everything together as a foursome, just like before.

In a busy church with a large congregation, it's difficult to get to know absolutely everybody. Each household tended to have its own rather elastic circle of friends, with a good deal of overlapping.

'Electric Fish' were joined on Sundays by musicians from other households and from none, to form a small orchestra of sorts which played during the services. By the spring, John and I had become rather concerned about our flautist, Sheilagh, a PE student from one of the church households. We hadn't known her awfully well, but we did notice that she was looking thin and very tired, and that she wasn't the delightfully spontaneous soul she had been in meetings.

One Sunday, Sheilagh picked up her flute to play along with us, but she was shaking so much that she had the greatest difficulty controlling her breathing and fingering.

After the service, we approached her gently.

'Sheilagh, what is it? What's wrong?'

It was nothing, she said. Then, no, it was everything. Apart from the pressure of 'finals', there were personality clashes within her household, and her parents couldn't understand her desire to stay in Durham even after she'd qualified, and as her 'community' family were moving away soon, she'd have to find somewhere else to live anyway.

We sympathized, we prayed with her, and we prayed for her. 'Lord, please show Sheilagh soon just where you want her to be after this college year.'

'Could she come to us?' I asked John later.

'It'd be difficult,' he said. 'She'd need a room of her own, and it wouldn't be for just a few weeks this time.'

But despite such logical thinking, we both felt slightly hypocritical, praying for a new home for Sheilagh without being willing to offer her one ourselves.

'OK,' John announced one evening, 'if it's just a case of the Lord testing our willingness, we'll ask her to come here. But I'm sure she won't want to. She'll almost certainly say no.'

But Sheilagh didn't say no. She threw her arms around each one of us in turn and said: 'I've been praying you'd ask me that! I simply hadn't the cheek to suggest it myself because I could see it would be a problem knowing where to put me. So I prayed: "Lord, if you want me to live with the Courties please make *them* ask *me*." And you did!'

In June we installed Sheilagh's bed in an alcoved corner of the boys' bedroom, behind 'walls' made of wardrobes and curtains.

In July Simeon 'invented' the periscope! Something had to be done!

A college couple just round the corner were moving out of their rented three-bedroomed house, and the owner kindly offered it to us for the remaining year of John's course.

Sheilagh's tension and nervousness didn't disappear overnight, however. Her parents, whom we all visited frequently, must have wondered whether she'd be better off at home with them, but were sensitive enough not to pressurize her. They understood that she felt the need at that time to establish herself as a person outside the parental home. But it was hard to see, in her first few months with us, just what good we could be doing her.

We all got pretty dispirited as the summer rolled on and Sheilagh hadn't been offered a teaching job. Her self-confidence was slowly ebbing away, and she became more and more withdrawn. Among our friends at church who were concerned for her was a local GP who was able to show his Christian love in a practical way. He suggested that Sheilagh work for him as a receptionist.

Although Sheilagh herself was more than a little apprehensive at the prospect, she agreed to give it a try, and we began to see a small, slow miracle. She learned to type from scratch, she mastered the complicated filing system, she developed a remarkable rapport with the patients, and confessed to actually enjoying her work. Gradually the inner healing began to show on the outside. Her eyes were bright again, she regained lost weight. Best of all she recovered her tendency to laugh out loud whenever she was struck by something ridiculous.

Very soon, Sheilagh was the happy and assured young lady we'd once known at a distance. Only we now knew her extremely well as the single 'addition' in our extended household.

Not everyone approved of our *ménage à trois*. Sheilagh's presence would certainly threaten our marriage, we were warned. Quite apart from the lack of emotional and spiritual privacy we'd suffer in having to include the otherwise isolated third party, taking in this particular third party was asking for trouble, they said. Well, just look at her!

Sheilagh was petite, pretty, fair-skinned, with clear blue eyes and very long naturally wavy blonde hair. In another culture she could have become a film starlet. But in our family she was more of a daughter, to begin with anyway. People did sometimes take her for the boys' big sister, which amused them if not their mother! Over the months, as we shared confidences, chores and cooking, she became less of a daughter in my eyes and more of a sister. The daughter/ sister I'd never had, perhaps.

There were occasional rows, when one of the three adults felt slighted or misunderstood, but we usually managed to talk and pray things through together. And because John and I had been married for ten years before Sheilagh came to us, we didn't find it too difficult to maintain our own particular unique relationship within the family.

Bob and Val, who might have been forgiven for distancing themselves from our new set-up, in fact did no such thing. They loved Sheilagh as much as we did and welcomed her as part of our old extended family and also as part of 'Electric Fish', where she sang with Val or played her flute.

Even the staff at Cranmer Hall were sympathetic to our

domestic arrangements. They allowed John to sign in for meals with three 'children'!

In our last months in Durham we were seven plus dog, albeit under two roofs.

Chloe grew old and stiff, but still smiled at half-remembered rabbit hunts.

Simeon at seven was perfecting methods of flying. Having long since mastered crawling, walking and running, this seemed to him to be the next logical goal, only adults, being stupid, had somehow overlooked it.

Gavin, although naturally shy, had discovered the Cub Scouts, and survived his first camp, arriving home dog-tired, black with grime, with a rucksack full of unused underwear and pyjamas, and in proud possession of his Cook's badge.

Sheilagh was pursued by every unattached male in the church but maddened them all by keeping them happily at arm's length.

Val, always uncomplicated and practical, was rectory secretary and unofficial parish diplomat.

Bob's boundless enthusiasm and optimism were engaged in seeking out a parish that might require two new curates and a band in one job-lot. Quite fruitlessly, as it happened.

By now, I was fairly accomplished in the art of surfacing with ease at different times in different hats — wife, mother, friend, student, musician. The studies had been profitable. I was now qualified to teach RE.

And John sorted us all out. He tuned the instruments and set the sound levels. He gee'd us up or calmed us down as required. And he infuriated us by being right too often for comfort. He also picked up an Honours BA and a theology diploma. But they were only part of his preparation for parish ministry. And perhaps not the most important part, at that.

Undoubtedly, though, the highlight of that last year was the arrival of Number Eight. This was Sarah, Bob and Val's adopted daughter. When she was baptized by the Principal in the college chapel, with Sheilagh, John and me as her godparents, we gave thanks to the Lord for this gift to all of us. Because whatever might happen to our 'household' after Durham, we knew that our combined nurturing of this newest member would serve to maintain the bonds between us all.

For all that, when Bob and Val left first, for a parish in Tyne and Wear, saying goodbye was hard.

As it turned out, we never did say goodbye to Sheilagh. She wanted to stay with us, she said, regardless of where we moved next.

And where we moved next was Liverpool. Again.

Chapter 9

✳ Liverpool: Same City, New Life

Like any major city, Liverpool is many-faceted. But perhaps more than any other city, her public image has been a persistent magnification of some of these facets at the expense of the rest. Liverpool *is* the Beatles, football, riots, unemployment, dying docks and Bleasdale's 'Boys from the Blackstuff'. But Liverpool is also greenbelt, gardens, theatre, concerts, enterprise, hope and humour.

The humour is all-pervasive, whatever your angle on Liverpool. The morning after the worst of the 1981 riots there were jokes rippling through the streets.

Police officer to youth with brick aimed at shop window:

'What's that you've got in your hand, lad?'

Youth:

'Er . . . a down payment on a video recorder!'

Apocryphal, no doubt. But it could just be true. The essence of Liverpudlian humour is never to be stuck for the last word.

I remember in the fifties the women selling flowers outside the main entrance of the old St John's Market, now demolished.

''Ere y'are, lucky heather, thrippence a bunch!'

The old dear stood with her basket at her feet, the obligatory black shawl clutched round her shoulders as she thrust handfuls of heather at passers-by.

She aimed a bunch at a very elegant lady who appeared not to notice.

''Ere y'are, luv,' persisted the flower seller, 'buy me lucky heather, an' good luck will foller yer all the days of yer life!'

The lady walked on without an acknowledgement, so the

old woman called after her, 'AN' NEVER CATCH UP WID YER!'

When we arrived at our particular leafy suburb in the summer of 1977, it was with a sense of joy and expectancy.

John was at his pre-ordination retreat at a nearby monastery, the boys were somewhere in the trees around the sandstone Victorian church, and Sheilagh and I were preparing our new home, in the servants' quarters of the vast vicarage, to receive the eleven overnight guests coming for the ceremony.

I was in the kitchen trying to stretch the crockery to cope with fifteen when she came in and announced: 'The loo doesn't flush.'

'Perhaps it needs a bit of time,' I said. 'Go back in a few minutes and give it another go.'

'I just did. The tank's not filling at all.'

'Well, lift the top off and jiggle something. That sometimes does the trick,' I suggested, without too much concern.

'Brenda,' she said earnestly, 'the plumbing's ancient, and the tank's twelve feet up the wall with a chain. A chain that won't flush!'

Before I could decide what to do, the phone rang and we both went through to the living-room.

It was John.

'You're supposed to be incommunicado!' I told him.

'We're allowed out for walks,' was the explanation, 'and I just happened to stroll towards this call box. How're things?'

'Oh, we'll be all right so long as we don't all have breakfast at the same time tomorrow!'

I felt a dig in my back.

'Tell him about the loo,' Sheilagh whispered.

'And the lavatory doesn't flush,' I said. 'It's very old, with a chain, and nothing's happening.'

The implications were beginning to get through to me as I put him in the picture.

'It could be a bit awkward with fifteen of us. Any ideas?'

'Can you keep a secret?' he asked, somewhat irrelevantly to my mind.

'Of course. Why?'

'I'll be home in ten minutes!'

A bit of wire did the trick and we were spared any embarrassment with our visitors.

After breakfast in shifts, we drove in convoy through the sunlit park to the city and the cathedral.

'It's just like Bournemouth!' claimed a friend from Wigan.

On that route it is. There are other routes, of course. Many facets.

The service couldn't fail to be moving, with those hundreds of people gathered in the great Gothic nave to watch the bishop ordain, set apart, a handful of men and women called by God to be his special servants.

I was moved. I was also a little distracted by my concern for those next to me.

The children watched intently, but how much could they understand of what Daddy was doing up there at the front, the bishop's hands now on his head?

John's parents watched, too. It was all so unfamiliar to them, this church business. Of course, it was an honour to see your son 'take the cloth', but with his brains, wasn't it a bit of a waste?

Even Sheilagh couldn't share my feelings. She'd only known John as an ordinand, training for this very event.

But for me, John's ordination was emigration. A journey to an unknown land.

Oh, we'd talked of the possibility for years, yes. Prayed about it, too, between ourselves and with others. I'd been spared the shock suffered by those wives whose husbands secretly leapt from office desk to altar without revealing a hint of any religious aspiration at home. And at least those women who marry fully-fledged clergymen do have some idea what they're letting themselves in for, and can look forward either to participating or leaving him to it.

John and I had prepared together for this journey, neither of us knowing exactly what it would be like. Now here we were. We'd landed in this other world, the ordained ministry. The man I married, the research student who went into teaching, was now a clergyman. How would I cope in reality with the terrain I'd only heard about second-hand? The public life, the people's expectations of me, the twenty four hour day, the low pay, the problems on the doorstep vying with the problems in the family?

John and I had always shared everything. How would I cope with being married to only half of him, while some other part of him cared and counselled and kept confidences?

To begin with, I didn't cope very well at all, despite enormous advantages.

Our church was in a very pleasant upmarket area, yet less than a mile from Toxteth where we'd lived all those years ago.

The local schools were excellent. After the summer break, Simeon went off happily to the nearest junior school, conveniently opposite the Anglican boys' school where Gavin now began his secondary education.

The church itself was buoyant, with numbers at the weekly Family Eucharist soaring above four hundred. The vicar and his wife, a couple of about our own age, were wonderful, and as we heard tales later of other 'mature' curates suffering under insecure and defensive incumbents, we thanked God for Ken and Margaret.

John was taken on as a colleague and given plenty of opportunity and encouragement to share and develop his own gifts. Both of us were gently urged to share our charismatic experience with the people. And, with Sheilagh, we were soon gathering around us sufficient musicians to form a small orchestra for some of the services.

But under the surface, so many adjustments had to be made, in so many different directions, and all at the same time. New schools, new friends, new job (though Sheilagh was unemployed, and that was a new experience, too), new church, new home.

I thought I'd been as prepared as I could be, and we were in a marvellous parish, so what was there to complain about?

'The six day week!' I wailed. 'Nobody warned me about the six day week!'

'Good heavens!' chided my elders and betters, 'Thousands of people work a six day week! Pull yourself together, girl!'

I didn't mind a bit that six days a week were given over to 'the job', morning, noon and night. I didn't mind living 'on the job', either. Actually, I found I liked that enormously, and pitied clergy families whose homes were some distance from their churches. I didn't mind the long Sundays which, for John at least, began before the eight o'clock communion and ended very late after the Sunday evening youth group. But with no spare time on the six working days, there was far too much non-work to squash into one day off.

We'd imagined our day off would be just that, a day in the country with a picnic lunch and games with the children. Exhibitions and museums on rainy days, perhaps. Idyllic! Except that we couldn't *not* visit John's parents, my relations, and old Liverpool friends who kept ringing us up to ask when were we going over?

We couldn't *not* take the children for shoes.

We couldn't *not* mend the car.

We couldn't *not* do the garden.

And we certainly couldn't *not* renovate the house.

Even without the house and its problems, our one day off was far more hectic than the other six days put together. Without a genuine day of rest we should have become totally exhausted in a very short time anyway. But it was the house that clinched it.

We were living in the wing of the vicarage which had once accommodated the domestic end of the household, the kitchen, pantry and scullery downstairs, and the day nursery and night nursery upstairs. The stairs were the original 'back stairs', of course, and they continued into the attics of the main wing, where the maids' rooms had been.

Over the years, the house had been very sensibly divided into three: the main vicarage, the curate's house with a new front door, and a flat in the vicarage attic. So the old kitchen was now our living-room, the scullery was our kitchen, and the pantry should have been a study, only Sheilagh needed a bedroom! Upstairs, the boys had the day nursery, and the night nursery had been divided into a small bedroom and a bathroom. This bedroom was now John's study, with a wall-bed that dropped down at night for the two of us.

The rooms in themselves were all quite large, so we didn't feel any lack of space. But there hadn't been a curate for years, and the house had received scant attention from the dozens of temporary residents, mostly students, who'd flitted through *en route* to better things. We were faced with the task of removing eight layers of cheerful lick-and-promise wallpaper, the most recent of which had been applied *around* somebody's furniture, leaving wardrobe-shaped gaps of older paper that our furniture didn't altogether hide! The kitchen was dark and depressing. The ceiling was all grease, and the floor (when we first saw it under the previous tenancy) all mouse droppings.

The two main sources of heat were a very small open fire in the living-room and a radiator on the landing, courtesy of the main vicarage system. This actually got hotter than any of the vicarage radiators, which seemed quite unfair, and led to jokes about the two families taking turns to sit round it!

We never did tackle the endless stair-well, but we redecorated the six rooms and the landing during our first five months in the parish. When I look back now, I see those rooms from the top of a step ladder.

As we were so very new, we held back from publicly wondering why the parishioners hadn't managed at least some of the work before our arrival as part of making us feel welcome. Though, to be fair, one of the church wardens had opened up a more convenient door into Sheilagh's pantry-bedroom.

Gradually we came to understand something of the arm's length attitude.

The vicar himself was a recent incumbent and, prior to his arrival, it had been the tradition of the parish not to interfere with the clergy! Even when invited, the local people had always felt that they shouldn't encroach on clergy territory. 'Dropping in' just didn't happen. There had to be reasons and proper appointments.

Because of the long years of such conditioning, very few parishioners even knew what the inside of either house looked like. And that meant that when we did finally persuade our new friends to cross the threshold nobody realized what a transformation we'd wrought!

After we left that parish, we heard that a team had gone in and totally redecorated the whole of our house in readiness for the arrival of the new curate and his family.

'Why couldn't they have done that for us?' I was to ask my husband. 'And anyway, it didn't need it. We'd done it all!'

'Of course they must do it,' John assured me. 'It's their gift to the new family. And their changed attitude is really a gift to us. That's better than pots of paint, isn't it?'

If I'd seen the end from the beginning it would have been easier.

In fact, John's enthusiasm for his new job seemed to counter his feelings of depression or frustration as we bashed on, but I gradually sank into a deep gloom. As I felt the waves of despair lapping at my feet, I fought like Canute to hold them back, carried daily to the water's edge by two gigantic fears. If I should succumb yet again to depression it would mean that my Faringdon illness wasn't just a result of my bereavement, Simeon's arrival, or simply physical sickness. I'd have no wreckage of justification to cling to. And if I had to admit I couldn't cope with being a clergy wife in our very first parish, it would mean John was saddled with a partner who was a hindrance, not a helpmeet.

Fortunately, although I was every bit as proud as old King Canute, I was spared his isolation. John was fully aware of my struggles, and he very gently persuaded me to talk to our new GP. It's perhaps easier to thank God for the splint that supports a fractured limb than for the medication that rests a tortured mind or soothes a wounded spirit. I was glad of our doctor's 'invisible splint', and grew strong enough to discard it after a few months when the tide had turned.

It was a relief, if not a surprise, to realize anew that while I was mortal and therefore subject to all of life's emotions, I certainly wasn't incurably neurotic. No. At the end of the course of tablets I was still me, even if the ticket in my hatband now said 'clergy wife'.

Most Anglican clergy wives are rounded up from time to time by their local rural dean's wife (if he has one) for clergy wives' meetings. Obviously, these vary from place to place, from life-saving to loathsome.

I once heard someone liken clergymen to manure. Very useful when spread thinly, but in a heap . . . !

There are some clergy wives who feel that way about clergy wives, but I'm not one of them. I was very fortunate to be taken to an 'underground' group of likeminded friends from all over the diocese who also happened to be married to clergymen. Every couple of months we'd meet at one of the homes, flop around on cushions, and eat a meal of curry or goulash or whatever, that we'd brought with us in bits and pieces. There was no 'leader', no rural dean's wife whose husband might not approve of our fun and games, our moans and groans or our little blasphemies. The therapeutic value of those times of total relaxation with people in the same boat who would be neither shocked nor hurt by my steam-letting is not to be guessed at.

Our church was attached to the university chaplaincy, and although the students had their own meetings, they came and mixed freely in the worship on Sundays, and we were glad to have several of them helping us with the music.

The church music group consisted of a selection of pianists, a clutch of guitars with me on bass, a trombone, a cello, a violin, a clarinet, some recorders, two flutes and a piccolo. Our student trombonist was also a fine tuba player and would occasionally borrow my instrument. Then our Sousa-cum-beergarden version of 'Follow Him, Follow Him' was a riotous roof-raiser not entirely out of place in the celebrations of the monthly parade service.

After rehearsing in the church on Sunday afternoons, the band and friends would gather for tea at our house, or in the garden on warmer days, and these lovely youngsters, so on fire for their Lord, impressed their enthusiasm and joy on my memory for ever.

While John dealt with the youth group on Sunday evenings, Sheilagh and I would take our tuba and flute to the Scout hut the other side of our garden wall, where a large jazz band, mainly ex-Scouts, met weekly. This was great fun too, simply because it *is* very funny trying to make sense of 'Tiger Rag' with musicians ranging from our volatile lead cornet ('I'm rubbish when I'm sober!'), to the willing beginner on tenor trombone ('Does a big round note with a hole in the middle count for two or for four?'). But somehow or other we managed to sort things out twice a year when we played jazz favourites at the Summer Tattoo, and carols for Christmas at the Athletics Club bar.

It seemed there was music wherever you turned in this parish. Even the ladies' meeting had a group that rehearsed regularly and staged an annual show. I got severely reprimanded by another clergy wife for my insensitivity in appearing as a Black and White Minstrel (I was a black one) with these ladies.

'You can't do that in this city!' she lectured. 'It's inflammatory!'

I suppose it depends how you look at it. Hers was the only complaint that came to our attention. The old folks' homes yelled for more, and the parish performances raised hundreds of pounds for city charities.

Perhaps all this music stemmed from the fact that our vicar was himself a music graduate. It was his setting of the communion service we sang each Sunday, and sometimes he would play piano with the music group. The only trouble then was that he loved extemporizing, and we'd hear chords and suspensions that weren't there before!

But Ken's talent for composition came into its own when we had a parish mission led by Bishop Richard Hare, for which he wrote some special songs, including a setting of the communion words:

> *Renew us by your Spirit,*
> *Inspire us with your love,*
> *And unite us in the body of your Son,*
> *Jesus Christ our Lord.*

It was a rather tentative mission. The dozen or so house-groups had under John's supervision become well-established growth cells following parish courses, but they were only the tip of the iceberg. What level of commitment was there amongst the hundreds of others who came regularly to worship on Sundays? The mission would encourage the committed, challenge the uncommitted, and provoke the complete outsider to some serious consideration. We hoped.

There were pre-mission prayer groups, lunches and teas, and the parish was flooded with glossy booklets illustrating the church's life.

Bishop Hare preached to well-filled pews every evening. There was special music, drama and dance, but no specific appeal was made. At least, not until the last evening.

'I think the best thing,' said the bishop before the final service, 'is for me to announce the last song "Renew us by your Spirit". I'll tell them that when it's finished the service will be over, and they can either go to the hall for a coffee, go home to their baby-sitters, or come up to the sanctuary if they'd like further prayer or help.'

This low-key arrangement was intended to allay any fears of 'emotional pressure'.

The bishop asked some of the house-group leaders to be ready to join him in the sanctuary to help counsel the people who might come forward, so when he'd made his little announcement about Ken's song I crept up into the darkened chancel and sat in a deserted choir stall to pray quietly during the singing. I had been a bit diffident about Ken's music when we'd rehearsed it. The harmonies were too romantic for my taste. But now, as I prayed, and the crowded church rang with the voices of people singing the words and meaning them, I realized I was wrong. In Ken's beautiful and adventurous harmonies, those words had met their match. I was very moved during that song, and walked back to the sanctuary when it finished, biting back the tears.

As I approached the altar rail I noticed a figure in the shadow of a pillar, well-hidden from the congregation. It was Graham, one of the leaders, looking most furtive. Then Bill, our Church Army captain, appeared beside him, and there followed much whispering and 'peeping out'!

Later, I discovered that Graham had been extremely reticent about joining the bishop's helpers in the sanctuary.

'I thought it looked a bit off-putting,' he said. 'So many of us up there, when I was sure there'd only be one or two coming forward. I thought if Bill and I kept hidden, people would be less embarrassed about the surfeit of ministers, and if we weren't needed we could creep off for some coffee!'

Dear Graham! His Christian humility often took the form of a shy apology and I loved him for it. Even after a week of stirring mission addresses from one of the Church of England's most remarkable preachers, he was far too polite to expect any miracles!

Bill persuaded Graham to take a quick peek. He did. And saw most of the huge congregation crowding into the centre aisle and surging forward towards the chancel where a queue was forming.

'Come on,' Bill urged. 'There's half the parish heading up here. The bishop needs some help!'

So Graham and Bill came over to the sanctuary, and ten or more of us prayed steadily with that stream of people for over an hour.

What struck me in the weeks after the mission was the number of husbands it had helped.

'Jean was always the real churchgoer,' said Don, typical of many, 'and she'd bring the kids, of course. But it only started to make sense to me personally at the mission. I mean this relationship with Jesus. I'm not sure whether Jean's pleased or not, because now we have to take turns going to the house-group, whereas before she'd go and I'd babysit!'

Lauren's teenagers were members of the parish youth group, but she'd been uneasy about coming to church herself after being divorced and remarried. Encouraged by John, she'd brought her husband Steve to a few social functions, and had ventured to church once or twice without him. All four of them knelt at the altar rail after the bishop's last address.

'Dorothy seemed to find the church a great comfort,' Ben told me. 'We'd both been very bitter after Emma [their Down's Syndrome baby] arrived. Then at a self-help group, Dorothy met Jim and Sally. You know, the ones with the two handicapped children. Well, they got Dorothy coming to church. I came a few times, too, and I liked the people and the services. But it was the mission that explained everything to me. That's why I went up for prayer. To tell God I trusted him for the future. Emma's future.'

He thought hard for a moment, then smiled broadly.

'You know, I wouldn't have missed that mission for a gold clock!'

And that really is about the way I think of our stay in our first parish.

It was grim at times, I know. Desolate, even. With our backs up against the wall we often snapped at one another, John and me, Sheilagh and me, John and Sheilagh. But our outbursts all said the same thing underneath.

'Help! I'm only little and the water's deep!'

But we learned to swim. Sheilagh learned to drive as well, got a job and bought a car! And we found ourselves helping others in their shallows.

When we said our tearful farewells in the end, at a special social evening, we were surrounded by scores of friends. Many of them had been brought to real faith through the mission, and it was particularly hard to say goodbye knowing we couldn't stay to watch them grow.

In three short years we'd come to love so many lovely people. We'd not only put down roots in this parish, we'd put out suckers, and untangling and tearing ourselves away was bound to hurt.

Your first parish is not only the place where you make all your first mistakes, all your first adjustments, as a minister or his wife. It's also the place where you start to see your first results, meet your first changed lives.

So your first parish is very, very special.

I wouldn't have missed it for a gold clock!

Chapter 10

✣ A Living on a Hill

I well remember my first encounter with oysters. It was during a family seaside holiday in France, and we had to resort to the contents of the car's toolbox before we finally got the knack of prising them open!

The Lord in his wisdom knew he'd have just as hard a job prising us out of our first parish. But as it's not in his nature to use a cold chisel and a lump hammer, he came up instead with an irresistible 'open sesame', in the form of a letter from our bishop, David Sheppard.

He asked John to consider becoming vicar of St Paul's, Hatton Hill.

'Do you know it?' asked John as we read the letter again over breakfast.

Did I know it!

My attention was suddenly caught by the sound of the little private aeroplane that flew every morning from Speke to Heaven-knows-where, and back again at teatime. Its sun-glint silver against the blue sky was as much a part of our mealtimes as the teapot on the tablecloth, and I looked straight through it to the Heaven of my childhood dreams.

Hatton Hill! That land of endless sunshine and birdsong, where the privileged residents were tempted away from their luxury homes by the click of the bowls on the greens or the mellowed wood quiet of the chapel interior.

'I knew it when I was very small,' I said, 'but I suppose it will have changed a lot over the years.'

It had, of course, and so had I. Houses with gardens, bathrooms and electricity were few people's Utopia now, and no longer mine. The little private estate around the park and the church had been overshadowed by four large council estates which had eaten into the countryside beyond the hill, and the population of 16,000 was served by two brick churches, the new St Paul's next to the former chapel, and the Roman Catholic church on the edge of the first new estate.

The new St Paul's was light and airy, but the church-wardens pointed out that its electric heating was inadequate and expensive. The roof leaked too, and not even the experts could say where or why. And in the hall, once the old church, there were signs of sad neglect and frequent vandalism, making the place more and more of a financial burden.

Still, they liked the look of John, and John liked the look of the parish, and when the two of us went to share our impressions with Bishop David, I was surprised to find that I was the one with reservations.

'A lot of people in the parish will know me,' I explained to the bishop.

Several old neighbours had been rehoused in the area. In fact, my own grandmother had only recently left an old person's bungalow in the parish, and there were still other relatives dotted about.

'Do you see that as a problem?' asked Bishop David.

'Well, yes, insofar as I'm not the person some of them will remember.'

'How do you mean?'

'It's like I've been rubbed out and redrawn since my childhood in Bootle,' I said. 'I was a scruffy little waif who went to grammar school and had her accent ironed out. I'm not really complaining. A lot of people were extremely kind to me, and I'm grateful for the opportunities I've had that others were perhaps denied. But I'm different now, because of all that.'

'And what worries you in particular?' pressed the bishop.

'I suppose I'm afraid they'll think I've acquired airs and graces, coming back married to a vicar!'

Bishop David knew exactly what I was talking about.

'Grace and I faced a similar dilemma when we lived in the East End,' he said. 'We found Bruce Kenrick's book *Come out the wilderness* tremendously helpful, and I'd pass on his advice to you. Be yourself, the 'yourself' you are now. Don't pretend to be anything else, not even the self you used to be.'

So with that very minor worry sorted out, we packed up and prepared to move.

The pain of leaving our old parish was lessened by the prospect of living in a roomy modern vicarage, built just before financial squeezes began to rule out nice touches like parquet floors and brass door and window fittings. The vicarage garden was something of a wilderness after our fruitful Victorian kitchen garden, but the house itself had great potential. I raced up and down new curtains on the sewing machine, and we went to a discount warehouse and spent our 'first living' grant on the necessary carpets and rugs and took them straight to the empty vicarage.

Then, the evening before our planned carpet-fitting day, the curate of St Paul's phoned to say he was very sorry to report that the vicarage had been burgled and all our carpets were stolen!

John, Sheilagh and I had a very despondent prayer-time, and Sheilagh disappeared into her little 'pantry' while John and I washed the supper things together.

A moment later, she bounded out again and dashed into the kitchen with an open Bible.

'Look at what was set for tonight in my notes!'

She smiled and read to us from the prophet Amos: 'I will restore the fortunes of my people Israel, and they shall rebuild the ruined cities and inhabit them; they shall plant vineyards and drink their wine, and they shall make gardens and eat their fruit.'

'Which I think means that things will be all right in the end even if they're hairy in the beginning,' John said with a sigh. 'We'd better make a note of that verse. I think we're going to need to remember what God has said to us about this move.'

Sheilagh copied it out on a slip of paper and pinned it to the kitchen wall, and we all went to bed feeling marginally better.

With the bishop's assurance that the diocese would reimburse us for the stolen carpets even if the insurance company didn't (in fact they did), we went to the discount warehouse yet again, and had to reassure the saleslady, who thought she was having a bad dream, taking exactly the same order from a clergyman who'd been in with the same details just days earlier!

The verse from Amos became our lifeline during our first weeks in the new parish.

A fortnight after the move, I went to a clergy wives' conference in Yorkshire, and while I was there John phoned me from home to say his father had died very suddenly.

'I'll come right away,' I said.

But he said no, there was nothing to be done, and I'd be coming home tomorrow in any case. Mother was coping as well as could be expected, and John would be toing and froing between the two houses each day.

'What about you? And the boys?'

'I'm all right, I think. A bit dazed, I suppose. But there's so much to do after a bereavement, you're kept very busy.'

I knew that was true. I remembered all the chasing round that followed my mother's death.

'Sim's had a good weep, but he's OK. It's poor Gavin who's had the worse jolt.'

'How d'you mean?'

'Well, when I told him about Grandad today, after he came in from school, he said he'd like to go for a long ride on his bike. I let him go, thinking it was a good way for him to digest the news. But when he went to get his bike from the garage it wasn't there. I'm afraid someone's pinched it while I was over at Mum's.'

That did it!

I hated, but hated with all my heart, the stinking God-forsaken social dustbin called Hatton Hill. How could I have thought it Heaven? Only Hell would steal a grieving grandchild's bike. I didn't care how many promises of prosperity there were in the Bible, Hatton Hill was beneath contempt and beyond redemption.

I went from the phone booth to the bathroom and threw up. Then I went to my room and wept. Only partly for Gran. Mostly for Gavin.

I was livid. I'd have said my fury was directed against the parish, but I know now I was angry with God. I also know now that I was genuinely upset by Dad's death, and hurt because Hatton Hill had shattered the long-cherished image I'd held of it.

But the words God spoke to Israel through Amos stayed pinned to our new kitchen wall, and as we were met time and time again by the sympathy and friendship of our churchpeople, the wound began to heal.

It would have healed faster, perhaps, if there hadn't been other much smaller irritations.

While Simeon settled happily into the local junior school, Gavin found the transition from his small church grammar school to the larger and much harsher comprehensive very difficult. Once again, as in Wigan years earlier, his southern vowels attracted ridicule, only this time it took more than a haircut and new trousers to appease his tormentors.

John and I realized the great lengths our son was going to in trying to identify with his peers, when he started playing football at lunchtime. He hated football! He'd always been bookish and had only tolerated games lessons. Of course, he came home with his shoes scuffed, his trouser knees muddy and his blazer elbows torn.

'Leave them, Mum,' he begged. 'Don't mend or wash anything. I blend like this!'

Our prayers for Gavin at this time sprang as much from guilt as from normal parental concern. It's all very noble, 'answering a call from the Lord', but the kids just have to up sticks, like it or lump it.

There were irritations on the church front, too. Some of the most earnest Christians in the congregation were soon fairly well convinced that God had sent them the wrong man! The new vicar's sincere faith, his testimony of conversion, his preaching of the gospel, his praying for the sick and his encouraging of the lay people counted for nothing, it seemed, once it was discovered that he wasn't strictly teetotal and didn't care a fig one way or the other if some of the church organizations held an occasional raffle for their funds.

Once we'd picked ourselves up after the initial barrage we assessed the situation as best we could. Several old factions within the church had apparently reformed during the interregnum in order to challenge the new man to dare align himself with the opposition!

Naturally, John refused to be any one group's commander-in-chief, and tried his best to take the heat out of all the 'party spirit'. But we had been 'weighed in the balance and found wanting'. Some people left the church right away, others withdrew their support while they waited for signs of our improvement, and one or two were conveniently offered jobs in different parts of the country.

I must say, for a long time I agreed with these dissenters. God *had* sent them the wrong man! Nothing seemed to have gone right since before we'd moved in, even, and I for one would gladly have packed my bags and gone back to our old parish! But to be fair, most of our people were a constant encouragement to us, urging us to ignore the criticisms as untypical and unworthy.

The Bible verse continued to speak to us daily from the kitchen wall, and fortunately we had other things to think about than dancing to the varying tunes of self-appointed pipers.

My grandmother, 'Nanny', was now very elderly and had gone to live with my aunt in a council flat in the next parish. It was lovely to be able to hop on my bike and pop off to see them at a moment's notice.

It soon became apparent that Aunty was quite worn out looking after the old lady, and it was arranged that I should stay at the flat and take over her duties while she took a short holiday.

Nanny had always been a very independent lady, and as the eldest child of eleven, whose own husband was more or less an invalid after the Great War, she had spent her life taking responsibility for other people's welfare. Consequently, she found it hard to be on the receiving end of the care and attention. I knew she could be very awkward with my aunt, but she was like a willing child with me, which was unfair but nice!

Only once that week did she make the blood drain from my face. We were going for a walk up to the garden bench at the front of the flats, and I'd got her down the tricky stairs when I realized I'd forgotten her walking stick.

'Just hang on to the railings, Nanny,' I said, 'I'll only be a tick.'

When I came back with the stick, she'd gone!

I looked round frantically. There she was, teetering about at the top of the road like a policeman directing the traffic!

'You took your time,' she scolded. 'I'm very nearly there!'

She was in a pensive mood another day after a difficult trip, involving both of us, to the bathroom and back.

'Why do you do it?' she asked.

'Do what, Nanny?'

'Help me like this.'

Poor dear! She was having such a hard time adjusting to the changed situation. I could have wept for her.

'It's what families are for,' I said, 'loving and caring. Who looked after me when my Dad died and my Mum went out to work?'

'I did, love,' she said, 'I did.'

'Well, Nanny, I'm doubly lucky. Because the Lord's given me the chance to help repay a tiny part of that debt. It's not often that that happens, you know.'

'I'm not always a good girl, though, am I?'

I smiled and gave her a playful nudge.

'I think you're sometimes very naughty and so does Aunty! But we know it's hard for you, and we love you, so don't you worry about it.'

She shuffled about in her high-backed armchair, sniffed and said: 'Anything on telly?'

End of conversation!

When Nanny died, her parish church was packed to overflowing for her funeral, and I counted four clergymen in the congregation. John preached on the text: 'I go to prepare a place for you.' He spoke with affection about the lady who, as cleaning woman and 'daily' to dozens of local people, had spent most of her days 'preparing a place' for others. She had sorted herself out with God at the late age of sixty, when she was confirmed, and now she was enjoying the bliss of a place specially prepared for her by her Saviour.

The tears were not confined to the family, I noticed.

Diversion of an easier kind came with a request to do some teaching at Simeon's school. The headmaster had to go into hospital, so all the staff moved up one and I went in as novice helper.

Juniors aren't really my forte. I'd done a bit of supply teaching at our junior school in Wigan, but as I'm trained to teach older children, I'd been relieved at that time to hand everything back to the regular teacher, and I moved instead to being 'stand-in' at the grammar school with John. But here I was back with little ones again. The other staff were wonderfully helpful, feeding me with ideas and projects, and I had a very enjoyable term teaching (if you could call it that!) everything from science to needlework. I'm sure I benefited more than the children, because within weeks I could recognize the local kids playing in the streets and greet them by name. And of course, I was soon bumping into their parents at the shops. These were links which would normally have taken much longer to forge.

Later, I did a term at a boys' public school, using my RE from Durham, and with the added 'lollipop' of an Oxford Entrance candidate from the girls' school.

Meanwhile, John was doing some teaching of a different kind. He was responsible for tutoring a group of first-year clergymen for their post-ordination training, the period of in-service supervision known throughout the Anglican church as 'potty training'!

At the end of his group's year, we gave a cheese and wine party for them and said our farewells. One curate, however, was not so keen to sever the connection, and before long was calling back on a regular basis. Not that his theology was in any way lacking. No, it wasn't John that Robert phoned and visited. It was Sheilagh!

Before long a wedding was planned which, in our calendar anyway, was to completely upstage the Royal Wedding which came a few weeks later. The church was filled with friends from up and down the country, and not a few dog-collars among them. The service was a joyful celebration with music, and dancing from the dance group Sheilagh had trained and encouraged in our first parish.

All her family came down from Sunderland, of course, and I was touched by the grace and warmth of her parents who showed no trace of disappointment or resentment that their daughter should be married from our home rather than theirs. And how proud her father was to be photo-graphed with the happy couple, surrounded by his entire brood, all now married, and their various children. It was the best outcome imaginable, and he could hardly have thought it possible when his poor confused daughter first came to us as a student.

At the end of the day, I watched the sunlight creep away from the clipped lawn and the neat flower beds we'd worked so hard at to get 'just right' for the wedding. And I remembered 'our' verse: 'They shall make gardens'.

The Lord was keeping his promises. Things were much brighter than when we first arrived.

John had an exhausting year on his own after our curate moved on to be vicar elsewhere, and it did seem for a while that there was never going to be another curate available for us. Our parish has a sort of daughter church, shared with the Methodists, on one of the estates, so the bishops were loath to send us a new deacon to do the lion's share up there. On the other hand, men who were mature enough to shoulder the burden quite naturally preferred to be a 'proper' vicar of their own parish.

After prayer, prayer, and more prayer, a phone call from an old Cranmer Hall friend ended our dilemma.

'I hear you're looking for a colleague. Can I come and talk about it?'

John had no hesitation at all in saying 'yes'.

What vicar would refuse the partnership of someone who has taught in Kirkby New Town, served in Kenya as a missionary for twelve years, then trained for the ministry and spent five years on a difficult inner-city estate? Here, certainly, was someone with invaluable experience at 'rebuilding ruined cities'.

But before all the loose ends could be tied, he thought he ought to sound out the church council about his new assistant. After all, some people might just object to the job going to a woman!

Ann, however, was not just any woman, or even any deaconess. Unknown to us, her parents were old friends of many of our church people, and our congregation had faithfully supported 'Olive and Joe's daughter' during her years abroad. Now they felt that God had rewarded their prayers by sending Ann to them as his own personal gift to St Paul's!

Ann's arrival also marked the beginning of a new musical venture for John and me. During the fun and games at the 'Welcome to Ann' social evening, we sang some songs with our organist and his wife, John and Ruth. Like us, they'd once sung with others in a group, and when the four of us got together with our guitars, we found we 'gelled' fairly well. Sunday evenings became practice nights at their house, when we'd work hard on new arrangements to sing at the old people's homes, church meetings or missionary rallies. It was good to be singing again. To sing songs to the Lord, or to others about the Lord, is a tremendous ministry and privilege explicitly encouraged in the Psalms.

When Ann's missionary society organized a big area rally at the Liverpool Philharmonic Hall, John and I were asked to round up a band and choir for the occasion. We'd been back in the city long enough by this time to know other Christian musicians in addition to John and Ruth, who shared our vision of the role of music in worship. As the great congregation gathered to praise God, we supplied a solid 'raft' of sound, secure enough to let the people relax and catch the wind of the Spirit, but with no aggressive tugging at their earlobes!

It helped, of course, that John and I were familiar with the concert hall from the scores of times we'd played there in the past with the Youth Orchestra and other ensembles. But this time it was quite different. It was more like our days in Durham with Bob and Val. We played and the people worshipped. It's a strange but lovely situation where people notice you less and less because they notice God more and more.

Music is perhaps one obvious branch of the 'ministry of deflection' as it might be called, where one is involved in an activity that helps other people in their relationship with God.

However, since leaving Durham, I'd found myself drawn, almost against my will, into quite a different aspect of this kind of work. And all because it's very hard to say 'no' to a bishop's wife!

Chapter 11

❈ Hello, Glad Tidings!

I'd always thought of music as being my 'thing', so it came as a bit of a surprise when my speaking voice caught the attention of Steve Henshall, wife of the Bishop of Warrington.

'You should do radio talks,' she said. 'You've got the voice for it!'

I must say I wasn't convinced.

'Oh, I think you have to have more than the voice. You need to have something to say, don't you?'

'Heavens! You'd have no trouble with that!' she insisted. 'If I can do it, I'm sure you can!'

I wasn't sure of any such thing. But Steve has a marvellous gift for cheerfully coaxing people into uncharted waters. Finally, I signed up for a training course run by the BBC and Chester diocese, where I learned many things.

First, I learned how to write and present a short religious talk. So far so good.

But I also learned that I had a hang-up about sounding 'big hat' and 'telephone voice'. (My grandmother had the most outrageous telephone voice, worthy of Wilde's Lady Bracknell!)

And I was quite unconvinced about exhorting people to get right with God over their cornflakes. I could see that an early morning dulcet-toned meditation might be a godsend to a lonely invalid, but I couldn't help wondering about the harassed mum with the breakfast and the baby and the kids who are dawdling instead of getting off to school. Or her husband, stuck in a traffic jam, knowing he'll be late for work. There are times when a 'holy joe' on the kitchen tranny or the in-car stereo is just one more irritation which, mercifully, can be switched off! I didn't want to get tied up in doing something, however 'worthy', that I just didn't believe in.

Then came the session featuring drama and humour in religious broadcasting. I knew and admired the work of Frank Topping on radio and television, but the idea of ordinary Christians doing that sort of thing on local radio hadn't occurred to me.

After the session I asked the lecturer: 'Are you serious? Do you want local people to have a go at that sort of thing, funny monologues and what-have-you?'

'I just wish I could find one local Christian bold enough to give it a try!' was his wry answer.

I said no more just then, but went off for a think and a pray.

Later that evening I sought him out and said: 'What do you think of The Woman at the Well in John's Gospel, happening today, in Liverpool?'

'Sounds good. Let me hear it.'

I looked again at my script for a minute, then admitted a difficulty.

'Er . . . it's a bit hard to get into it in a vacuum. Can I grab a couple of people to be the friends I'm supposed to be talking to?'

'Feel free!'

I found two 'friends', and he set up his tape-recorder.

Then somehow, I just became that poor woman, outcast, immoral, but sensitive and defensive. And I lapsed without effort into my native Liverpool dialect, which seemed to add not just humour, but pathos.

When I'd finished we sat in silence for a moment or two. Then the lecturer said: 'I was hoping for something like that. Do you know you have a real gift for timing? Forget the other stuff. You concentrate on this sort of thing. It's good.'

Following the course, I did a series of six Bible incidents, updated into contemporary Liverpool, which were broadcast on BBC Radio Merseyside. So I was 'in' on religious broadcasting, though not doing quite what the bishop's wife had expected.

The use of dialect led to an unexpected spin-off when a secular producer asked me to do some freelance reading for his short story programme.

'It's rare to find someone who can switch from standard English to genuine Scouse,' he explained. 'Usually I have to choose between drama school English with genuine Scouse, or standard English with drama school Scouse!'

'Oh, my Scouse is genuine,' I assured him. 'You can't be born and bred down by the Bootle docks and not have the language.'

I considered telling him about the other vital talent of the bomb-sites that I was also master of. But I reckoned the ability to whistle loudly through my fingers wasn't such a marketable commodity. Well, not on radio, anyway!

However, it wasn't long before I realized that the memories from my childhood were eminently marketable. I'd been reading some 'nostalgia' pieces sent in by local writers, and after the recording session I asked Reg, the producer: 'Do you get a lot of stuff like this?'

'Tons of it,' he answered as he rewound the tape. 'Of course, they're not always particularly well-written.'

I knew that. It was very much easier to read the better ones. But they were local, which made them interesting.

I sat quietly as he listened to the first few seconds of the playback.

'That'll do!' he smiled, and he took off his headphones.

'What about you?' he asked while he wrote some brief details on the yellow leader tape. 'Was yours an interesting childhood?'

'You wouldn't believe it!' I told him.

Reg tossed the completed tape into a basket.

'Then write about it. And let me see what you write.'

So I did. I wrote a description of our house by the docks, some stories about Marj and me, tales of parties in the streets and bonfires in the streets, and my memories of the 1951 Festival of Britain.

Reg liked them enough to use them on his programme, and they prompted him to offer me some advice.

'Join a writers' circle,' he said, and he gave me the name of a contact near my home. 'And of course, you ought to write a book.'

'A *book*!' I echoed, and I laughed. 'Oh, I can't see me doing that!'

But I did find the writers' club, and quickly picked up enough to realize that magazines publish freelance 'nostalgia' articles. I sold two in swift succession, then went on to try my hand at 'Women's Page' articles for our provincial daily newspaper. These too were accepted, and as I was now reading my own totally fictitious short stories on local radio I realized I'd been well and truly bitten by the writing bug.

Soon, I was scribbling away at not one book, but three! The romantic novel got off to a good start, but was shelved in favour of a humorous 'vicarage' novel. And then that got shelved when my present publisher showed an interest in using my own true story. And all the time I was still sending off articles to various magazines.

When the editor of a national religious weekly phoned and asked me to cover some news stories, I knew that my writing could be more than an enjoyable hobby. Here I had a home-made new career, a part-time job I hadn't looked for, a job I could do in my own time from the vicarage.

In the meantime, my religious talks were taking a change in direction. Obviously, there's a limit to how many Bible stories can be reset in modern Liverpool and still retain their credibility. I'd already 'cheated' by telling the story of the Cripple at the Pool of Bethesda as if I were a friend of the family, a fictional woman who of course doesn't appear in the Bible account.

It was an easy transition, though, from that role of observer to the role of a local Scouse Christian housewife, who talks about her husband, her children and the state of her world, in the familiar Liverpool tongue, laced with plenty of humour, and with a clear and simple Bible message tucked in somewhere. We called her 'Mrs Gladys Tidings'. Glad Tidings to her friends!

After a gentle introduction now and again over a period of weeks, and a temporary 'ban' while it was decided whether or not she was lowering the tone of the station's religious broadcasting, Gladys was finally given a regular Saturday morning slot.

The feedback was mixed. Everything from 'Isn't it a pity that your vicar's wife is so common?' to 'I've never laughed so much in my life but it did make me think'.

Of all my bits of writing, the 'Glad Tidings' talks are both the easiest and the hardest.

I can sit down and scribble the words: ''Ello! Yerrit's me, Gladys. Glad Tidings', and immediately I'm in character and can prattle on in my native tongue for pages and pages. But of course that's not the point of the exercise. It's the religious slot I'm supplying, so I have to discipline myself to carefully selecting a message and letting Gladys discover it or explore it in her own way.

Then I hone it down until the words that are left are only there because they help to convey the message to the listener in the two minutes and thirty seconds air-time.

By the time I get to the recording studio (I usually record four talks at a time, and the tapes are used on appropriate days) all the hard work is finished.

Once again, the words ''Ello! Yerrit's me, Gladys' throw the switch in my mind, and I 'talk' the script to my imagined single listener as if the two of us were in my kitchen having a cup of tea.

When people complain, as they do sometimes, that common and ignorant people like Gladys shouldn't be allowed to talk about religious topics in such a humorous and therefore disrespectful way, I don't get too discouraged. It means I've done a good job as a writer at least, and 'you can't see the join'.

I do get a bit bothered, though, by complaints from people who realize that when I'm on the radio I'm in fact acting a part, but who think I shouldn't. Along with modern Bible translations, revised hymns and 'the new Prayer Book', I'm accused of devaluing Christianity by bringing it down to the lowest common denominator.

Such criticism saddens me slightly, because that's not my intention at all. All I'm trying to do, via Gladys, is to communicate the gospel of Jesus in a particular way for particular people.

Our deaconess, Ann, once went to a great deal of trouble to learn Kikuyu so that she could communicate the gospel to people in Kenya who found formal English hard going. There are people in Liverpool who find formal English hard going. I think it makes good sense to speak to them in their own language. And I didn't even have to learn it!

Sometimes I use Gladys scripts as part of a talk at women's groups, and there's usually someone who comments on the complete switch of role and voice.

'You sounded so different!' they'll say. 'I couldn't believe it was the same person!'

But then that's the whole point. I'm playing a part. Or am I?

I think perhaps Glad Tidings is my alter ego. The 'myself' I'd like to have been, if life had dealt with me differently. If I hadn't come to Hatton Hill married to its vicar.

Chapter 12

❊ Not Quite Heaven, But . . .

'Yes, but what else do you do?'

People are usually intelligent enought to guess that a vicar's wife does a bit more than don a big hat and open the local fête. And perhaps they are curious enough to wonder sometimes, just what else does she do? But few, I think have either the opportunity or boldness to voice the question in so many words.

There isn't a standard answer anyway, because no two 'VWs' are the same.

Whereas most church ministers of most denominations spend most of their time doing the things they were all similarly trained to do, things like prayer and study, visiting, baptisms, weddings, funerals, services, counselling and meetings, their wives have to work out their own role for themselves, according to their outlook and their particular situation.

This in itself would be difficult enough, even if the VW were able to sit down and think about it rationally. But most times, she doesn't get the chance to decide for herself: 'I think I'll help with this, but I don't think I'd quite fit in with that, and I'm sure I shan't have time for the other.'

I've been pretty lucky in our two parishes, but I know from others what often happens. From the day her husband is appointed to his parish, indeed from some time before if she's been brave enough to go with him to meet the church council, the VW is bombarded by outside pressure as to what her role ought to be.

First of all, there's the outright lobbying by the church people.

'Your wife will run the Mother's Union, won't she,

vicar? Oh, and the pram club. Oh yes, and the playgroup.'

Sometimes the shots are less direct, but they still hit the mark.

'You do realize, don't you, that only the Vicar's Wife can do the sanctuary flowers?'

'Sorry about the tatty magazine. Our last vicar's wife used to type the stencils so beautifully.'

'But our last vicar's wife *always* took the Sunday School!'

There are VWs up and down the country who reckon that if ever a species ought to be exterminated from this planet, it's that harridan-cum-paragon, 'The Last Vicar's Wife'!

Certainly, it's very hard to resist being pressed into the gap left by the LVW. But that's nothing compared to the outside criticism and inside guilt faced by some VWs who are bold enough to pursue their own careers. I was once greeted with all kinds of heartfelt apologies by the leader of a church women's group where I was to be the guest speaker.

'Oh, Mrs Courtie. I'm so sorry. My name's Mrs Smith. I'm afraid *I'm* the leader here these days. Unfortunately, our new vicar's wife goes out to business!'

The slightly lowered voice indicated the enormous iniquity being hinted at!

The truth is, I suppose, that most parishes even these days would still prefer their vicar's wife to be his unpaid full-time assistant. However, some VWs feel quite different pressures upon them.

There are, in fact, clergy wives who can't afford to work for nothing. Their families need a second income. Why? Because a vicar is paid less than the national average wage (he's usually on a par with a farm labourer), and some families have extra commitments that can only be met out of the wife's salary.

For example, many clergy couples try to buy a home of their own ready for their retirement. Some protect their children from the trauma of school transfers with father's moves, or from the bewilderment of a hostile environment (particularly in the cities), by sending them to boarding schools.

I've enjoyed the part-time teaching jobs that have come my way occasionally since John was ordained, particularly the RE ones, but I much prefer being around at home and in the parish. Indulging this preference does mean some material sacrifices for my family, however.

Stretching the monthly cheque to cover mortgage on the retirement house, car repayments, food and general household expenses takes a bit of doing. We sometimes use the fees from weddings or funerals to buy clothes, but you have to be careful about this because this year's fees are knocked off next year's stipend. I must say, I find jumble sales are a godsend!

Our vicarage comes free, of course, like the farm labourer's tied cottage. But vicarages are generally a good deal larger than farm cottages and so cost a lot more to run and to heat. In summer, we've got our retirement house (a tiny terrace in a Lancashire mill town) for free holidays. Other more conventional holidays, if they happen, come as gifts from friends or are financed by church charities.

So although every vicarage family has its own way of making the money go round, there's no denying that a second income makes it a lot easier.

Apart from the Last Vicar's Wife, then, and the material needs of her own family, what other influences can govern a VWs role?

Well, the vicarage itself is something of a pressure cooker! It's not only the clergy home, it's also the clergy office, the clergy waiting room, the clergy consulting room, the clergy meeting room and the clergy guest house. And where is the staff to service all these facilities? Ah, she comes free with the vicar . . . if he's married.

In addition to looking after her family and a large house and garden on a small income, in the gaps the VW will also brew endless cups of tea and coffee for meetings, visitors or tramps, rustle up extra meals for guest speakers, returned missionaries or confirming bishops, and sort out beds for any of these who might be staying for a time.

While her husband is out doing services or visiting in the parish, she will also answer the phone and the doorbell.

A peephole gadget in the front door will give you some idea what, or who, to expect, but with the phone you never know. I've often wished they'd invent a telephone that would flash the caller's number as it rang!

Prepared for anything, then, the VW rubs the pastry off her hands and deals with a new consignment of oil for the church hall, or several small boys with a 'present' of half a ton of newspapers, or a phone enquiry about a baptism, or the undertaker with details of yet another funeral, or the very angry father whose teenage daughter has run away, or the very sad lady who says she's going to go and take two bottles of sleeping pills. Right now!

And on a bad day, it all happens at once!

Of course, every caller rightly expects a particular and appropriate response, which means that the poor VW is switching from sympathy to congratulations, from bustling efficiency to patient understanding, almost minute by minute.

No wonder some clergy wives would rather be out at work!

So what about me? Why don't I get back into full-time teaching and leave the phone ringing in an empty house?

I suppose there are three reasons.

Top of the list is what you might call shared ministry or sheer nosiness depending on how you see it. I just like being involved with John's work. As lay people we took on church tasks together. As schoolteachers we taught in the same schools. We prayed together for years about his call, ordination and training. So now, whatever credit or blame is attached to us being here (opinions differ, even within the household!), I was part of the getting here. I'd find it hard not to be part of the being here.

Apart from that, we've found that as a family we don't function terribly well when I go out to work. My approach to life's chores is to leap single-mindedly from project to project (or from crisis to crisis; again, opinions differ!). So while I'm loading up my bike with a chart of the Old Testament prophets the size of a barn door, someone upstairs is bleating: 'My football kit didn't get washed!'

The last reason is less easily defined. It's not at all a general principle, and it probably wouldn't impinge on me in other circumstances. I'm just not sure that I could handle the guilt I think I'd feel if I were earning more than my husband in an area where so many homes haven't even one income, let alone two. I'd be fearful of confirming the 'landed gentry' image that still blights middle-class clergy in working-class parishes. But that's just me.

Anyway, despite all the pressures and stupid irritations, I'm actually quite happy with my lot. I enjoy being a Vicar's Wife.

I don't mean the awful kudos that almost makes you 'The Rev. Mrs Bloggs'. I came across something of that soon after we arrived here, when I was invited to a ladies' prayer meeting.

'Just come as you are. It's very informal. Round at our house for a time of prayer and a cup of tea.'

I went on my bike, in my dungarees, and was the youngest member attending. But I wasn't allowed to help with the tea, and when it was brought in, I wondered why I'd been served with a china cup and saucer when the ladies either side of me had mugs.

'Oh, but *you're* the *Vicar's Wife*!'

I'm glad to say that this is now an old joke and today I get a mug along with all the rest! So, no, it's not the kudos I enjoy.

And it's not just the 'working with people' part, either. The great procession of parishioners that parades daily through our vicarage is not just a social worker's case-list.

I think of the parish more in terms of a tapestry. God is

using the many different threads to make a unified and harmonious picture, eventually, only we can't see it yet. John is perhaps the needle, pushed and pulled this way and that, by a force outside of himself, as he takes the threads the way they must go for the picture to be right.

And me?

Something of a sewing monitor, I think. Looking after the bits and pieces. Keeping my eye on the needle. Untangling some of the threads, and tidying up the knots on the back where nobody sees.

It's not quite Heaven these days up here on Hatton Hill. They've boarded up the pavilion in the park to keep the vandals out and most of the swings are broken. But you can still hear the click of the bowls on the greens on a summer afternoon.

And I've discovered other wonders now, not dreamt of when I coveted electric light and lollipops. Deep things, like a trust in God's sovereignty, a peace with myself and a hope beyond all darkness. Things God himself has taught me over the years, and is teaching me still.

Things I might not have found if I'd come up the short way.